BACON
24/SEVEN

BACON
24/SEVEN

RECIPES FOR CURING, SMOKING, AND EATING

THERESA GILLIAM

PHOTOGRAPHS BY EJ ARMSTRONG

THE COUNTRYMAN PRESS
A division of W. W. Norton & Company
Independent Publishers Since 1923

AUTHOR
Theresa Gilliam

ART DIRECTION & PHOTOGRAPHY
EJ Armstrong

COVER DESIGN
Alicia Nammacher

INTERIOR DESIGN AND COMPOSITION
Xiaonan Wang

RECIPES & FOOD STYLING
Theresa Gilliam

For information about permission to reproduce selections from this book, write to
Permissions, The Countryman Press, 500 Fifth Avenue, New York, NY 10110

For information about special discount for bulk purchases, please contact
W. W. Norton Special Sales at specialsales@wwnorton.com or 800-233-4830

The Countryman Press
www.countrymanpress.com

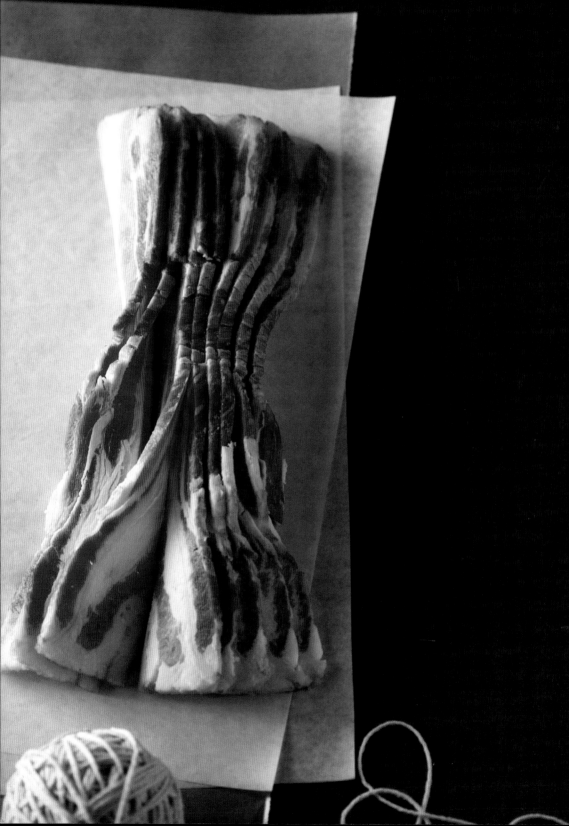

CONTENTS

FOREWORD

Life is better with bacon.

It is a universal truth on par with the laws of gravity: bacon makes things better.

Throughout this volume we will expound on this theory with recipes like Bacon Baklava (page 179) and Clarified Bacon Fat (page 22) in pie crust. We will guide you through the adventure of curing and smoking your own bacon at home.

The glory of bacon is how it stimulates all of the senses. Salt and fat mingle with sweetness, smoke, and crunch. It is a primal ingredient, a staple from our remembered palate. It recalls days of feasting and celebrations after months of toil. It deserves so much more than to stand guard over a plate of scrambled eggs.

BACON 101

The beauty of bacon is in its utter simplicity; a pork belly cured for 1 week, and then gently smoked with a flavorful wood for several hours. It is a sublime combination of salt, smoke, and heat that carries with it a plethora of culinary wonders.

Bacon 24/7 is our ode to American bacon. Yet even American bacon has a glossary of varieties available on the market.

GREEN BACON is cured but not smoked.

UNCURED BACON is often cured using the naturally occurring nitrates found in celery powder and then smoked.

WET-CURED BACON is soaked in a brine before smoking.

DRY-CURED BACON is rubbed with a dry salt mix before smoking.

There is also variety in both the cut and flavor of bacon as well. Whether you are shopping at your local grocery store or visiting an artisan butcher, you can find anything from slab bacon, thin-cut, thick-cut, maple-flavored, peppered, applewood smoked, hickory smoked, and more.

Use your favorite cut, flavor, or brand and seek out the best bacon you can find. There are a few recipes where we may recommend using peppered bacon or a thin-cut bacon because we like the flavor or the texture it provides for that particular recipe, but the philosophy of *Bacon 24/7* is that cooking doesn't necessarily have to be an exact science, so we leave it up to you.

Now that you have purchased or smoked your own bacon (pages 17–19) let's talk about how to cook it. Nearly every recipe in the book calls for a crispy cooked bacon. There are three schools of thought on cooking bacon; the conventional oven method, the microwave oven method, and the stovetop method. Refer to the basic cooking instructions on page 12 when cooking bacon. It is important to remember that the bacon will continue to cook and crisp up after it is removed from the heat for another minute or two, no matter what cooking method you are using. For better results, bring bacon to room temperature before cooking, then place bacon in a room temperature skillet or oven before turning on the heat. This will ensure that the bacon heats up slowly, maximizing the amount of fat rendered out of the bacon and will prevent scorching. Bacon can quickly go from perfectly crisp to charred and inedible. So whatever cooking method you choose, it's important to keep a close eye on it. It is also important to mention that cooking times may vary depending on the thickness, fat ratio, and water content of the bacon you are using.

CONVENTIONAL OVEN METHOD:

Place a wire rack on a foil-lined, rimmed sheet pan. Lay slices of bacon flat on top of the rack without overlapping. Place pan on the center rack of a cold oven and turn the oven to 400°F. Cook bacon for 20 to 25 minutes. There is no need to flip the bacon. Transfer cooked bacon to paper towels.

MICROWAVE OVEN METHOD:

Lay 4 to 5 slices of bacon in a single layer without overlapping in a microwave-safe dish, such as a glass baking dish. Cover with paper towels. Microwave on high for 4 to 5 minutes or 1 minute per slice. Flip the bacon slices and continue cooking in 1 minute increments until done to your liking. Transfer cooked bacon to paper towels.

STOVETOP METHOD:

Place bacon in a single layer in a large frying pan or cast iron skillet. It is okay to overlap the slices a little bit as they will shrink down with cooking. However, do not overcrowd the pan or you will steam the bacon rather than fry it. Place the pan over medium heat and cook about 4 to 5 minutes per side, turning often with a pair of tongs. Transfer cooked bacon to paper towels.

PAR-COOKED BACON:

Place two layers of paper towels on a microwave-safe plate. Lay desired amount of bacon in a single layer on top of paper towels and cover with three additional paper towels. Microwave bacon for 2 to 2½ minutes, or 30 seconds per slice.

HOME-CURED AND SMOKED BACON

To truly immerse yourself in a lifestyle bordering on obsession, it is essential to venture into the world of home-cured and smoked bacon. Armed with a raw pork belly and a few specialty items, you may find yourself never purchasing store bought bacon again. With a little time, patience, and the guidance provided in this chapter, you will be a week away from enjoying your greatest culinary endeavor.

SOURCING INGREDIENTS:

Good bacon starts with a good cut of pork belly. Keep in mind that most grocery stores don't carry large slabs of pork belly. However, most specialty butcher shops should carry, or be able to special order, a 2½ pound pork belly with the skin and ribs removed.

CREATING THE CURE:

To ensure that no harmful bacteria will grow during the curing process, it is important to use pink curing salt, also known as Prague Powder #1. This can be ordered online or purchased from specialty food shops. The pink curing salt used in the following recipes contains 6.25 percent sodium nitrite. There are those who have concerns about nitrites, but it is not harmful in small amounts.

It is also worth noting that not all kosher salts are the same. The following recipes were made using kosher salt containing 480 mg of sodium per ¼ teaspoon, such as Morton's.

It is tempting to skip the resting steps after the pork belly is removed from the cure, but it is important for the meat to be dry and not too cold before adding it to the smoker. If the meat is cold and wet, it will not take the smoke well and all your time and hard work will be wasted.

SMOKING A CURED PORK BELLY:

It is possible for most home cooks to smoke bacon no matter what kind of grill they have. The key is cooking at a low temperature over indirect heat. There are a few tools available that will make the process easier but are not essential.

You can smoke your bacon with just about any type of wood. The most common are hickory and applewood, but pecan, maple, or cherrywood are good options too. You can use wood chunks, wood chips, or food-grade wood pellets depending on your method and the type of smoker you are using. If you are using wood chips or chunks, you will need to soak them in water before use. There is no need to pre-soak wood pellets.

For indirect cooking with gas grills: Fire up one side of the burners to medium-low and leave the other side off (your target temperature is between 200°F–225°F). It is handy to have a stainless steel or cast-iron smoker box for your wood chips, which can be found online or at your local hardware store; however, a perforated pouch made of heavy-duty aluminum foil will also work. Place the smoker box or aluminum pouch filled with pre-soaked wood chips directly over the flames, under the cooking grate if possible. Once the grill is preheated and the wood begins to smoke, place the pork belly on the grill over the unlit burners so that no direct flames come in contact with the meat. Keep the lid closed as much as possible.

For indirect cooking with charcoal grills: Place a pile of burning charcoal off to one side of the grill and leave the other side bare (your target temperature is between 200°F–225°F). It is helpful to have a chimney charcoal starter. This will make replenishing dying coals much easier when the time comes and prevent the loss of precious heat and smoke while the grill is uncovered. Smoker boxes and aluminum pouches can be used directly on the burning coals, as well as pre-soaked wood chips and chunks (see previous paragraph). When using wood chips directly on the coals, be careful not to add too much at once or you will extinguish the charcoal. Replenish the wood chips whenever the smoke seeping from the grill begins to dissipate. Keep the grill covered as much as possible.

For electric, charcoal, or pellet smokers: Follow the manufacturer's instructions.

CURING RECIPES
Makes 2 pounds of bacon

Classic Cured Bacon

2½ pounds pork belly, skin and ribs removed
¼ cup light brown sugar
2 tablespoons kosher salt
1 tablespoon juniper berries, coarsely chopped
1 teaspoon pink curing salt
1–2 bay leaves, crushed

In a small mixing bowl, combine sugar, kosher salt, juniper berries, curing salt, and bay leaves to create a curing rub.

Sweet Cured Bacon

2½ pounds pork belly, skin and ribs removed
¼ cup light brown sugar
¼ cup maple sugar
2 tablespoons kosher salt
1 tablespoon pasteurized apple cider vinegar
1 teaspoon pink curing salt

In a small mixing bowl, combine brown sugar, maple sugar, kosher salt, vinegar, and curing salt to create a curing rub.

Spicy Cured Bacon

2½ pounds pork belly, skin and ribs removed
¼ cup light brown sugar
2 tablespoons kosher salt
2 tablespoons red pepper flakes
2 tablespoons cracked black peppercorns
1 tablespoon hot smoked paprika
1 tablespoon cayenne pepper
1 teaspoon pink curing salt

In a small mixing bowl, combine sugar, kosher salt, pepper flakes, black peppercorns, paprika, cayenne, and curing salt to create a curing rub.

Savory Cured Bacon

2½ pounds pork belly, skin and ribs removed
¼ cup light brown sugar
2 tablespoons kosher salt
1 tablespoon fennel seeds
1 tablespoon coriander seeds
1 tablespoon cumin seeds
1 teaspoon pink curing salt
1–2 bay leaves, crushed

In a dry skillet over medium heat, toast fennel seeds, coriander seeds, and cumin seeds until fragrant and just beginning to brown, about 2 to 3 minutes, stirring constantly. Coarsely grind in a spice grinder.

In a small mixing bowl, combine sugar, kosher salt, ground spices, curing salt, and bay leaves to create a curing rub.

For Curing and Smoking the Bacon:

Place pork belly on a baking sheet or large pan and rub generously on all sides with curing rub. Take a few minutes to vigorously massage the cure into the meat so that it is completely covered. Place pork belly in a large resealable bag. You may want to double bag to avoid leaks.

Refrigerate pork belly for 7 days, turn the bag over once a day and give it a gentle massage. It will accumulate liquid and will begin to feel firm to the touch.

After 7 days, remove the pork belly from the bag and discard the cure. Thoroughly rinse the pork belly under cold water to remove any excess curing rub or spices

and pat dry. Place on a rimmed baking sheet or pan and refrigerate, uncovered, for at least 8 hours and up to 24 hours.

While the cured pork belly is drying in the refrigerator, begin soaking wood chips or wood chunks in a bowl of cold water for at least 8 hours and up to 24 hours.

Remove cured pork belly from the refrigerator and allow to rest at room temperature while you prepare the smoker.

Preheat the grill or smoker to 200°F using the indirect method explained in the chapter introduction. Smoke cured pork belly for 2½ to 3 hours, or until internal temperature reaches 150°F. Remove from the smoker and cool completely.

Slice and cook bacon using your favorite method (page 12). To make slicing the bacon easier, place it in the freezer for 15 minutes before slicing. The bacon will keep in the refrigerator for 1 week, or in the freezer for 3 months.

CLARIFIED
BACON FAT

Throughout *Bacon 24/7* you will note that some recipes call for Clarified Bacon Fat. We hope that you haven't been throwing away this precious commodity! Of course not. You are a true bacon aficionado. The culinary possibilities reach far beyond what is called for in this book. Use it to fry eggs, sauté greens, cook vegetables, toss into pastas, make Southern fried chicken, or use it instead of shortening in baked goods. However, bacon fat does have more saturated fat, cholesterol, sodium, and calories than butter, so use it with discretion.

Makes about 1 cup clarified bacon fat

1 cup fresh, rendered bacon fat
2 cups cold water, divided

Strain rendered bacon fat through a fine mesh strainer into a small saucepan. Add 1 cup of water and bring to a boil over high heat. Reduce heat to medium and gently boil for 1 to 2 minutes. Transfer to a heat-proof container and add the remaining cup of cold water. Refrigerate for at least 5 hours until the fat has solidified, or freeze for 2 hours. The mixture will separate into a layer of clarified fat, a very thin layer of fat mixed with impurities, and a layer of water. Remove the solidified fat, shave off any impurities, and discard the water. Place clarified bacon fat in an airtight container and store in the refrigerator for up to 1 month, or in the freezer for up to 6 months.

TENDER AND FLAKY PIE CRUST

The combination of butter and bacon fat creates the perfect texture everyone strives for in their pie dough. This crust doesn't taste bacony so it can be used for both sweet and savory recipes.

Makes 2 (9-inch) pie crusts

3   cups all-purpose flour
¾   teaspoon salt
¾   cup (1½ sticks) unsalted butter, chilled and cut into ½-inch cubes
4   tablespoons Clarified Bacon Fat (page 22) softened
1   teaspoon apple cider vinegar
3–5 tablespoons ice cold water

In a food processor or in a large bowl using a pastry cutter, blend the flour and salt together until combined. Add the butter and fat and blend until the flour resembles a coarse meal. Stir in the vinegar. Add the water, 1 tablespoon at a time, until the the dough comes together and holds its shape without crumbling. Form dough into two disks, cover with plastic wrap and refrigerate for 30 minutes. Use as needed. The pie dough keeps for up to 2 days when refrigerated and up to 1 month when frozen.

To prebake the crust:

Preheat oven to 350°F. Line a 9-inch pie plate with pastry. Trim off the excess and decoratively crimp the edges. Pierce the bottom of pie all over with a fork. Chill pie shell for 30 minutes. Line the shell with parchment paper and fill with pie weights or dried beans. Bake for 15 to 20 minutes. Carefully remove the weights and parchment paper and bake for an additional 10 minutes until the edges have started to brown. Cool completely.

DAWN

DAWN

BACON AND RED PEPPER STRATA

A strata is like a breakfast casserole. This version is marvelous for brunch or to feed a crowd for a weekend gathering. It can be completely assembled the night before so the rich egg custard soaks into the bread, then it takes less than an hour to bake. Leftovers are great warmed up in the toaster oven.

Serves 6–8

6	slices peppered bacon, cut into 1-inch pieces
1	red bell pepper, sliced (about 1 cup)
2	cups sliced white or crimini mushrooms (6 ounces)
2	cloves garlic, thinly sliced
6	large eggs
2½	cups whole milk
½	cup heavy cream
½	cup thinly sliced chives
1	tablespoon chopped fresh oregano
1	tablespoon chopped fresh rosemary
1	tablespoon chopped fresh thyme
½	teaspoon salt
½	teaspoon freshly ground black pepper
1	loaf rustic French bread (1 pound), cut into ½-inch-thick slices
2	cups shredded Fontina

Cook the bacon in a large skillet over medium heat until crisp, about 8 minutes. Transfer to paper towels, reserving rendered bacon fat in the skillet.

In the same skillet, cook the bell peppers, mushrooms, and garlic over medium-high heat until softened and beginning to brown, about 4 minutes. Stir in reserved bacon and remove from heat.

Spray a deep 9-by-13-inch baking dish with cooking spray and set aside.

In a large bowl, whisk together the eggs, milk, cream, herbs, salt, and pepper.

Use half of the ingredients to create the first layer. Arrange the bread slices on the bottom of the prepared baking dish, distribute the bacon, pepper, and mushroom mixture over bread and sprinkle with shredded cheese. Pour half of the egg mixture evenly over the first layer. Repeat with the remaining ingredients for the second layer, finishing with all of the remaining egg mixture. Cover and refrigerate for at least one hour or overnight.

Preheat oven to 350°F. Bake uncovered for 45 to 50 minutes or until the egg is set and the top is beginning to brown and bubble.

Let stand 10 minutes before serving.

BACON CHEDDAR BISCUITS

These biscuits may be fluffy, but they are hardly what you would call delicate. They are sort of the "work horse" of the biscuit world. Enjoy them alone, slathered in our Bacon Redeye Gravy (page 40) or create the ultimate breakfast sandwich. For variation, add chives, sliced green onions, or use shredded Gruyere or Pepper Jack in place of the Cheddar.

Makes 6 biscuits

2   cups all-purpose flour
2   teaspoons baking powder
¼   teaspoon salt
1   cup shredded Cheddar
⅓   cup cooked and crumbled
     bacon (about 4 slices)
1½ cups heavy cream

Preheat oven to 425°F.

Line a baking sheet with parchment paper.

In a large bowl, whisk together the flour, baking powder, and salt. Stir in the cheese and bacon until it is evenly distributed and coated with flour. Stir in the cream until the dough is just moistened, about 30 seconds. Do not over mix.

Turn the dough out onto a lightly floured surface and gently knead until it is just smooth, about 30 seconds. Pat the dough into a rectangle, 1 inch thick. Cut the dough with a biscuit cutter into 3-inch rounds, or use a knife to cut it into 3-inch squares. Place the biscuits on the prepared baking sheet, 2 inches apart.

Bake for 15 to 18 minutes until golden brown.

*Over-the-top bacon lover's tip:

Before putting the biscuits in the oven, brush with a little melted Clarified Bacon Fat (page 22).

BACON REDEYE GRAVY

Redeye gravy was originally just a cup of coffee tossed into the skillet to catch the flavorful bits leftover from frying-up ham. This is our bacon-take on the Southern staple. Espresso adds an extra kick. The gravy is best served warm with Bacon Cheddar Biscuits (page 37), but is also nice with fried chicken or pork chops.

Makes about 2 cups

6   slices bacon, coarsely chopped (about 1½ cups)
2   tablespoons all-purpose flour
2   shots (2 ounces) espresso or ½ cup strong black coffee
1   cup whole milk
¼   cup heavy cream
¼   teaspoon salt
¼   teaspoon freshly ground black pepper

Cook the bacon in a large skillet over medium heat until crisp, about 8 minutes. Transfer to paper towels, reserving rendered bacon fat in the skillet.

Strain the rendered bacon fat through a fine mesh sieve to remove any charred bits. Return 2 tablespoons of the strained bacon fat to the skillet and warm over medium heat. Whisk in the flour to form a roux. Cook the roux to a golden brown, stirring often, about 2 minutes.

In a separate bowl, combine espresso, milk, and cream together. Gradually add the milk mixture to the roux, whisking constantly. Add the salt, pepper, and reserved bacon.

Simmer, stirring often, until thickened, 3 to 5 minutes. Serve warm.

FRIED GREEN TOMATO BENEDICT WITH BACON HOLLANDAISE

A Southern-inspired eggs Benedict with a double hit of bacon makes this a more-than-satisfying brunch favorite. Timing is everything with this recipe: the fried tomatoes are best eaten fresh out of the pan, but getting the muffin toasted, the egg poached, and the hollandaise on deck at the right time will take all your time management skills. The end result is well worth the effort. And why not serve it with a Bloody Hell Bloody Mary (page 56)?

Serves 2–4

For Fried Green Tomatoes:

¼ cup all-purpose flour, divided
¼ cup cornmeal
1 large egg
¼ cup buttermilk
1–2 green tomatoes
½ teaspoon salt
¼ teaspoon freshly ground black pepper
¼ cup vegetable oil

For Bacon Hollandaise Sauce:

2 egg yolks
2 tablespoons fresh lemon juice
½ teaspoon Dijon mustard
¼ teaspoon salt
1 pinch cayenne pepper
⅓ cup clarified butter, melted (homemade or store-bought)
2 tablespoons minced cooked bacon

For Assembly:

2 English muffins, halved and toasted
4 poached eggs
4 slices cooked bacon

For Green Tomatoes:

In a small bowl, combine 2 tablespoons of the all-purpose flour with the cornmeal. Set aside. Place the remaining 2 tablespoons of flour in a separate bowl and set aside. In a third bowl, whisk together the egg and buttermilk until well combined.

Slice the green tomato crosswise into ½-inch-thick slices. Pat dry and season both sides with salt and pepper.

Begin heating oil in a heavy skillet over medium heat as you prepare the breaded tomatoes.

Take one slice of tomato and dredge both sides in flour. Shake off any excess flour and dip the tomato in the egg mixture until completely coated. Shake off excess egg mixture and dredge both sides in the cornmeal mixture. Transfer to a plate and repeat breading process with remaining tomato slices.

Fry tomatoes in prepared skillet 2 minutes per side, until golden brown and crispy. Transfer to a paper towel–lined plate and keep warm.

For Bacon Hollandaise:

In a blender, place egg yolks, lemon juice, mustard, salt, and cayenne pepper. Blend until well combined, 10 to 15 seconds. With the blender running, slowly add the clarified butter in a steady stream. Add minced bacon and pulse just until combined. Serve immediately or keep warm until ready to serve. If the sauce becomes too thick, whisk in warm water one tablespoon at a time until it is desired consistency. Makes ½ cup.

For Assembly:

Place one Fried Green Tomato slice on a toasted English muffin half. Top with one slice of cooked bacon, folded in half. Top bacon with poached egg and 2 tablespoons of Bacon Hollandaise Sauce. Serve immediately.

*Over-the-top bacon lover's tip:

Add up to a tablespoon of Clarified Bacon Fat (page 22) to the Hollandaise sauce when adding the clarified butter. You will need to add a tablespoon of warm water as it with be a thicker consistency than when using just clarified butter alone.

QUICHE LORRAINE

You may have guests begging you for your secrets to making this classic preparation. What will you tell them? Will you share the fact that you used two kinds of Swiss cheese? That it is heavy cream that makes the custard so rich and fluffy? We know that the bacon-fat-enriched Tender and Flaky Pie Crust (page 29) is the real secret, but we will never tell!

Serves 6–8

1	prebaked 9-inch Tender and Flaky Pie Crust (page 29)
¾	cup cooked and crumbled bacon (about 8 slices)
1	cup shredded Gruyere (about 3 ounces)
1	cup shredded Jarlsberg (about 3½ ounces)
4	large eggs
1	cup milk
1	cup heavy cream
1	teaspoon fresh minced thyme
½	teaspoon freshly ground black pepper
¼	teaspoon salt

Preheat oven to 375°F.

Fill the pie shell with bacon and shredded cheese, tossing gently to combine. In a medium bowl, whisk together eggs, milk, cream, thyme, pepper, and salt. Pour the egg mixture over the filling.

Bake until the egg filling is puffed up and starting to lightly brown on the top, 20 to 25 minutes.

Cool for 10 minutes before serving.

MAPLE BACON TWISTS

We have to thank the geniuses at Voodoo Doughnuts in Portland, Oregon, for inspiring these sweet dreams intertwined with a strip of thick, salty bacon, all drizzled with a glaze made with real maple syrup. It's almost too good to be true. You may need to clear your schedule for a month or two so you can make these EVERY weekend.

Makes 12 doughnuts

⅓   cup warm water (110°F)
¼   cup granulated sugar, divided
1⅛   teaspoon yeast (½ packet)
1   large egg
3   tablespoons buttermilk
1¾   cups all-purpose flour
¼   teaspoon ground cinnamon
¼   teaspoon freshly grated
     nutmeg
⅛   teaspoon salt
12   slices thick-cut, maple-flavored
     bacon, par-cooked (page 12)
Peanut or canola oil, for frying
Maple Glaze (recipe follows)

In the bowl of a stand mixer, combine the water, 1 tablespoon of sugar, and yeast. Let the mixture sit for 10 minutes to activate the yeast. Whisk in the remaining sugar, egg, and buttermilk. Add the flour, cinnamon, nutmeg, and salt. Knead the dough with the dough hook attachment until well combined, about 3 minutes. The dough will be very sticky.

Transfer the dough to a large bowl coated lightly with cooking spray. Cover, and leave in a warm, draft-free place to rise until doubled in size, 1½ to 2 hours.

Transfer the dough to a floured surface and pat or roll it into a 1-inch-thick rectangle, approximately 8 by 12 inches. Cut the dough into 12 (1-by-8-inch) rectangular pieces with a pizza cutter or sharp knife.

Lay a slice of bacon on top of each piece of dough and twist 2 to 3 times to form a spiral, pinching the ends to adhere dough and bacon. Repeat with the remaining bacon and dough pieces. Cover and let rest for 30 minutes.

Preheat oil in a deep fryer or large pot to 350°F.

Deep fry the doughnuts, a few at a time, until the dough is fully cooked and the bacon is crisp, about 3 minutes. Transfer to a sheet pan lined with paper towels.

Drizzle the doughnuts with Maple Glaze and let the glaze set before serving.

MAPLE GLAZE

1½ cups powdered sugar
¼ cup maple syrup
2 tablespoons milk
1 teaspoon vanilla extract

Sift the powdered sugar into a medium bowl and whisk in the maple syrup, milk, and vanilla until smooth. Transfer to a piping bag or squeeze bottle or cover until ready to use.

GINGERBREAD BACON WAFFLES

These fluffy, yet substantial waffles have the flavor of a rich molasses cookie. The bacon adds an extra complexity and cuts the sweetness just the right amount.

Makes 10–12 waffles

3 cups all-purpose flour
2 teaspoons baking powder
2 teaspoons ground cinnamon
2 teaspoons ground ginger
1½ teaspoons baking soda
½ teaspoon salt
4 large eggs
⅔ cup packed dark brown sugar
1½ cups buttermilk
¼ cup molasses
½ cup (1 stick) butter, melted
8 slices Candied Bacon (page 170), chopped
Cooking spray or melted butter, for cooking

Preheat waffle iron and oven to 200°F.

In a large bowl whisk together flour, baking powder, cinnamon, ginger, baking soda, and salt. In a medium bowl, beat eggs and brown sugar with a whisk until combined, then beat in buttermilk, molasses, and melted butter. Stir the wet ingredients into the dry ingredients until just combined. Do not overmix. Gently fold in chopped Candied Bacon.

Coat waffle iron liberally with cooking spray or melted butter and cook waffles according to manufacturer's instructions. Serve immediately or keep warm in the oven until ready to serve. Serve with your favorite toppings, such as maple syrup and whipped cream.

*Over-the-top bacon lover's tip:

Brush waffle iron with a little melted Clarified Bacon Fat (page 22) before cooking the waffles.

BACON RICOTTA
CORN CAKES

These moist, flavorful pancakes are particularly delicious topped with a poached egg for breakfast or brunch. They are also fabulous served at dinner alongside ham or grilled salmon. They are as easy to make as any pancake, and are best served straight from the griddle for a perfect crisp exterior.

Makes 16 (4-inch) cakes

1   cup frozen sweet corn kernels, thawed
2   large eggs
15   ounces ricotta (about 2 cups)
1   cup whole milk
1   cup all-purpose flour
1   cup cornmeal
¼   cup granulated sugar
2½   teaspoons baking powder
½   teaspoon baking soda
½   teaspoon salt
½   cup cooked and crumbled bacon (about 6 slices)
Cooking spray or melted butter, for cooking

Pulse the corn in a food processor to a coarse puree. Add the eggs, ricotta, and milk and pulse until just combined.

In a large bowl, whisk together the flour, cornmeal, sugar, baking powder, baking soda, and salt. Make a well in the center of the dry ingredients and pour in the corn mixture. Stir to combine in just a few strokes. Fold in the cooked bacon.

Heat a griddle over medium heat. Coat liberally with cooking spray or melted butter. Spoon ⅓ cup of the batter onto the hot griddle and cook until golden brown or crispy, about 2 minutes per side. Repeat with the remaining batter.

Serve the corn cakes immediately or keep warm in a 200°F oven until ready to serve.

Top with poached eggs, if desired.

*Over-the-top bacon lover's tip:

Brush griddle with a little melted Clarified Bacon Fat (page 22) before cooking the pancakes.

BACON STUFFED FRENCH TOAST

Consider this for a decadent start to a lazy weekend or maybe a celebration feast after an active or productive morning. The orange adds a natural sweetness, so no syrup is necessary. Serve hot with a simple dusting of powdered sugar and perhaps a scattering of fresh berries.

Serves 4

6	large eggs
½	cup heavy cream
1	tablespoon orange zest
¼	cup granulated sugar
2	tablespoons orange liquor (optional)
½	teaspoon vanilla extract
½	teaspoon ground cinnamon
½	teaspoon freshly grated nutmeg
¼	teaspoon salt
8	slices brioche, ¾ inch thick
½	cup mascarpone, divided
8	slices thin-cut bacon, cooked (page 12)

Cooking spray or melted butter, for cooking

Powdered sugar and fresh berries, for garnish (optional)

In a shallow dish, whisk together the eggs, cream, orange zest, sugar, orange liquor (if using), vanilla, cinnamon, nutmeg, and salt.

Spread each slice of brioche with 1 tablespoon of mascarpone. Divide the bacon evenly among four slices of bread. Break off any extra bits of bacon to ensure that nothing hangs over the sides. This helps the bread slices to seal nicely. Brush the inside edges lightly with egg mixture and sandwich the bacon slices with the remaining bread slice. Press gently to seal the edges.

Working one or two at a time, dip the sandwiches in the egg mixture. For best results, leave the sandwiches to soak for a moment or two, then flip and soak the other side.

Preheat a large nonstick skillet or nonstick griddle over medium-low heat. Spray liberally with cooking spray or brush with melted butter. Slowly cook the sandwiches until they are golden brown, about 5 minutes per side. Serve immediately or keep warm in a 200°F oven until ready to serve.

Garnish with powdered sugar and fresh berries.

*Over-the-top bacon lover's tip:

Brush griddle with a little melted Clarified Bacon Fat (page 22) before cooking french toast.

BLOODY HELL
BLOODY MARY

There are multiple stories about who created the original bacon Bloody Mary. The battles about who was first or what recipe is best have been contentious and slightly sordid. This version is a total bacon bust that includes bacon vodka, Bacon Salt™, and a bacon twist garnish. It is so flavorful, you theoretically don't even need to add the booze—but in all honesty, the booze-less variety has yet to be tested. J&D's Bacon Salt is available online or at specialty food stores. If necessary, bacon flavored vodka, such as Bakon™ can be special ordered at your local liquor store.

Makes about 3 cups

2 tablespoons Worcestershire sauce
2 tablespoons freshly squeezed lemon juice
1 teaspoon prepared horseradish
½ teaspoon hot sauce, such as Tabasco brand
¼ teaspoon celery seed
¼ teaspoon ground coriander
¼ teaspoon freshly ground black pepper
¼ teaspoon salt
2 cups (16 ounces) tomato juice
½–¾ cup (4–6 ounces) bacon flavored or plain vodka
2 tablespoons Bacon Salt, such as J&D's brand
Lime wedges
Bacon Twists, for garnish (recipe follows)

In a large measuring cup or pitcher, combine the Worcestershire sauce, lemon juice, horseradish, hot sauce, celery seed, coriander, pepper, and salt. Add the tomato juice and vodka and stir well. Refrigerate until ready to serve.

Prepare four (8-ounce) drink glasses by rubbing the rim with a lime wedge and dipping in the Bacon Salt. Fill each glass with plenty of ice and divide the Bloody Mary mixture evenly among the glasses. Garnish each glass with a bacon twist and a lime wedge and serve immediately.

BACON TWISTS

4 slices thin-cut bacon
4 disposable wooden chopsticks

Preheat the oven to 425°F.

Wrap a piece of bacon around each chopstick in a spiral. Place the chopsticks on a rack over a foil-lined baking sheet. Bake until the bacon is brown and crispy, 15 to 20 minutes. Cool completely before gently removing the chopstick from the bacon.

FATSO CORNBREAD

Don't fight it! Embrace the decadence and slather each dense, moist, and slightly spicy slice generously with Whipped Honey Butter.

Makes 1 (5-by-9-inch) loaf or 1 (9-inch) round

2   tablespoons Clarified Bacon Fat (page 22)
1½ cups yellow cornmeal
1   cup all-purpose flour
2   teaspoons granulated sugar
2   teaspoons baking powder
½   teaspoon baking soda
½   teaspoon salt
2   large eggs
1½ cups buttermilk
2   tablespoons unsalted butter, melted
1   jalapeño pepper, seeded and minced
¼   cup cooked and crumbled bacon (about 3 slices)
Whipped honey butter

Preheat oven to 425°F.

Place a 9-inch cast-iron skillet or a standard loaf pan in the oven, coated with the Clarified Bacon Fat. Preheat while you assemble the cornbread, about 5 minutes.

In a large bowl, whisk together the cornmeal, flour, sugar, baking powder, baking soda, and salt. In a separate bowl, whisk together the eggs, buttermilk, and melted butter.

Make a well in the center of the dry ingredients. Pour the wet ingredients in, all at once. With a wooden spoon, gently stir the wet ingredients into the dry ingredients until well combined. Fold in the minced jalapeño.

Remove the hot pan from the oven and brush the hot, melted fat evenly on the sides and bottom of the pan. Pour in the batter. Sprinkle bacon on top. Bake until a toothpick inserted near the center comes out clean, 25 to 30 minutes.

Serve warm with whipped butter, if desired.

WHIPPED HONEY BUTTER

½   cup (1 stick) butter, at room temperature
3   tablespoons honey

Combine with an electric mixer and whip until light and fluffy, about 3 minutes.

BREAKFAST HAND PIES

This is an entire breakfast in one succulent little package of pastry. Use our bacon-fat-enriched Tender and Flaky Pie Crust (page 29) or your favorite commercial brand. Serve these straight from the oven with sour cream and salsa, or freeze them for a quick, midweek breakfast on-the-go.

Makes 6 (3-by-6-inch) hand pies

3   slices bacon, coarsely chopped (about ¾ cup)
1   large Yukon Gold potato, peeled and chopped (½-inch cubes)
½   cup shredded Monterey Jack
3   large eggs
1   tablespoon whole milk
1   jalapeño pepper, seeded and minced
¼   teaspoon salt
¼   teaspoon freshly ground black pepper
1   recipe of Tender and Flaky Pie Crust (page 29) or 1 (15-ounce) package store-bought pie dough
Salsa, sour cream, and fresh cilantro, for serving (optional)

Preheat oven to 450°F.

Line a baking sheet with parchment paper.

Cook the bacon in a large skillet over medium heat until crisp, about 8 minutes. Transfer to paper towels, reserving rendered bacon fat in the skillet.

In the same skillet, add the potatoes and cook until they are golden brown and tender, stirring occasionally, about 10 minutes. Transfer potatoes to a bowl with reserved bacon and cheese. Toss to combine.

In a medium bowl lightly beat the eggs with the milk. Stir in the minced jalapeños, salt, and pepper.

In the same skillet over medium-high heat, cook the egg mixture to a loose scramble, about 2 minutes.

Add the cooked egg mixture to the bacon, cheese, and potatoes and stir gently to combine. Set aside to cool while you prepare your pastry.

Roll out the pie dough on a lightly floured surface and cut into six (6-inch) rounds. You may need to gather up the scraps and re-roll the dough to form enough rounds.

Divide the filling evenly among the dough rounds. Moisten the edges of the dough lightly with water. Fold the dough over the filling to create half-moon shapes and press the edges to seal. Use the tines of a fork or your fingers to crimp the edges. Cut three small slits on top of each hand pie to allow steam to escape.

Arrange the pies on the prepared baking sheet and bake until golden brown and puffed, 15 to 20 minutes. Serve the hand pies hot with salsa, sour cream, and chopped cilantro, if desired.

FRIDAY'S FRITTATA

Frittatas are wonderfully adaptable. Slices of this family-size omelet can be served hot or cold for breakfast, lunch, or dinner. Hemingway put frittatas in between slabs of country-style bread for hearty sandwiches. This flavorful version might be best if it goes right in your mouth.

Serves 4–6

4 slices bacon, coarsely chopped (about 1 cup)
1 small onion, diced (about ¾ cup)
1 clove garlic, minced
8 cups baby spinach, washed and drained
1 tablespoon butter
6 large eggs
3 tablespoons milk
¼ teaspoon salt
¼ teaspoon freshly ground black pepper
2 tablespoons minced fresh chives
¼ cup shredded Parmesan
Sour cream and hot sauce, for serving (optional)

Place oven rack in the middle of the oven and preheat the broiler.

Cook the bacon in a large skillet over medium heat until crisp, about 8 minutes. Transfer to paper towels, reserving rendered bacon fat in the skillet.

In the same skillet cook the onion and garlic until softened, about 5 minutes. Transfer the onion mixture to a bowl. Cook the spinach in the skillet until it is wilted and tender, about 2 minutes. Work in batches if necessary. Transfer the cooked spinach to a colander and squeeze out as much liquid as possible. Chop the spinach and add it to the onion and garlic mixture.

Melt the butter in a large, oven-proof skillet over medium-high heat. In a bowl, whisk the eggs, milk, salt, and pepper together and pour into the skillet. Gently stir in the spinach, onion, bacon, and minced chives. Cook until the eggs are almost set, about 5 minutes, occasionally lifting up the edges of the frittata and tilting the pan so the uncooked egg mixture flows underneath. Sprinkle cheese over the top of the eggs and place the skillet in the oven. Broil until the frittata is set and the cheese begins to brown, about 3 minutes.

Cut the frittata into wedges and serve immediately with sour cream and hot sauce alongside.

MIDDAY

MIDDAY

ALSATIAN TART

This French onion tart is a wonderful party dish that appeals to a diverse crowd. It is great cut into tiny bites to serve with chilled white wine before an elaborate meal, or as slices served with cold beer for the big game.

Makes 1 (10-by-12-inch) tart

2　tablespoons olive oil
1　large onion, thinly sliced
½　teaspoon salt
½　teaspoon freshly ground black pepper
2　tablespoon white wine
1　sheet frozen puff pastry, thawed
½　cup (4 ounces) crème fraîche
8　slices par-cooked bacon (page 12) chopped (about ¾ cup)
¼　cup shredded Gruyere
¼　cup shredded white Cheddar
Egg wash, made with 1 egg yolk blended with 1 teaspoon of milk or water

Preheat oven to 400°F.

Heat the olive oil in a large skillet over medium heat. Add the onions, salt, and pepper and cook, stirring occasionally, until they are soft and golden brown, about 15 minutes. Add the wine and stir gently to dissolve any flavorful brown bits from the bottom of the skillet. Simmer until the wine is evaporated, about 2 minutes. Remove the skillet from heat.

Line a baking sheet with parchment paper.

Roll out the puff pastry on a lightly floured surface into a 10-by-12-inch rectangle. Transfer the dough to the prepared baking sheet. Spread crème fraîche evenly over the dough, leaving 1 inch of space around the edge. Sprinkle evenly with the chopped bacon and onions. Top with the shredded cheeses. Fold the exposed edges of the dough over the tart filling to form a 1-inch border. Gently press the corners to help seal the edges into place. Brush the exposed crust with the prepared egg wash.

Bake the tart until the crust is golden brown and the bacon is crisp, 20 to 25 minutes. Cut into 6 to 8 slices and serve hot.

BACON AND APPLE GRILLED CHEESE PANINI

Get your sandwich press out of the back of the cupboard (or the garage) and prepare to fall in love with it all over again. Manchego is a full-flavored, firm Spanish cheese that melts marvelously. Use a good aged Gouda for nutty complexity. But, let's face it, most any good cheese will make a divine sandwich when paired with crisp bacon and slices of tart apple. The Dijon adds a nice peppery tang. If you do not have a panini press, grill the sandwiches slowly on a lightly oiled griddle or skillet, about 4 minutes per side.

Serves 4

1   loaf of foccacia or ciabatta bread, cut into 4-inch squares
4   teaspoons Dijon mustard
1   Granny Smith or similar tart, firm apple, thinly sliced
1   cup shredded Manchego (about 3 ounces)
1   cup shredded Gouda (about 4 ounces)
12 slices of thick-cut bacon, cooked (page 12)

Slice the bread squares through the middle to make top and bottom slices. Spread 1 teaspoon of Dijon mustard on the top slices. Divide cheeses, apple slices, and bacon evenly among the bottom slices. Assemble the sandwiches and grill in a countertop grill or panini press according to manufacturer's instructions, until the bread is crisp and brown and the cheese is melted. Serve immediately.

FRISÉE SALAD

This is a variation on a classic French bistro salad. While the traditional version is topped with a warm poached egg, ours has baked slices of baguette slathered with goat cheese. The dressing should be warm but not too hot, so it very lightly wilts the slightly prickly leaves of frisée. It's sometimes helpful to make a double batch of glazed pistachios. They tend to disappear.

Serves 4

2 tablespoons extra virgin olive oil
8 (1-inch-thick) slices of baguette
4 ounces fresh goat cheese, softened
4 slices bacon, coarsely chopped (1 cup)
¼ cup red wine vinegar
1 head of frisée, rinsed, cored, and torn into bite size pieces
Freshly ground black pepper
Glazed Pistachios (recipe follows)

Preheat oven to 425°F. Line a baking sheet with parchment paper.

Brush olive oil evenly on both sides of the baguette slices. Spread the tops with 1 tablespoon of goat cheese. Bake on the prepared sheet pan until the edges are golden brown and the cheese begins to bubble, about 6 minutes. Keep warm while you prepare the salad.

Cook the bacon in a large skillet over medium heat until crisp, about 8 minutes. Turn off the heat. Add the vinegar, frisée, and black pepper to taste in the skillet and toss to coat. Serve the salad immediately on individual plates with two pieces of baguette and a sprinkling of Glazed Pistachios.

GLAZED PISTACHIOS

½ cup raw pistachios, shelled
1 tablespoon butter
1 tablespoon granulated sugar
1 tablespoon water

Melt the butter in a small skillet over medium-high heat. Add the pistachios. Sprinkle in the sugar and toss with the pistachios to coat, stirring constantly, about 2 minutes. When sugar begins to caramelize, add water and stir until sugar liquefies and coats pistachios. Transfer nuts to a piece of foil or parchment to cool.

POWER LUNCH
SPINACH SALAD

This is a well-balanced entrée salad rich in protein and omega-3 fatty acids. Serve it alongside grilled salmon and you can have your bacon and "power foods" all at the same time!

Serves 4

8   cups (6 ounces) baby spinach, rinsed and dried
1   cup cooked and crumbled bacon (about 12 slices)
1   cup thinly sliced mushrooms (8 ounces)
1   medium carrot, shaved into thin ribbons with a vegetable peeler
½   cup crumbled goat cheese (about 2½ ounces)
1   large avocado, diced (about 1 cup)
½   cup chopped, toasted walnuts
2   hard-boiled eggs, quartered lengthwise
Walnut Dressing (recipe follows)

Divide the spinach among four salad plates. Evenly distribute the bacon, mushrooms, carrots, goat cheese, and avocado among each serving. Top with walnuts and garnish with two pieces of egg. Drizzle the salads with Walnut Dressing and serve immediately.

WALNUT DRESSING

¼   cup champagne vinegar
1   tablespoon Dijon mustard
1   clove garlic, minced
2   teaspoons minced shallots
2   teaspoons chopped Italian parsley
½   cup walnut oil
Salt
Freshly ground black pepper

In a small bowl, combine the vinegar, mustard, garlic, shallot, and parsley. Add the oil in a slow, steady stream, whisking constantly to emulsify. Do not add the oil too quickly or the dressing will separate. Season with salt and pepper to taste. Keep refrigerated until ready to use.

POTLUCK
POTATO SALAD

Inspired by German-style potato salads, the potatoes soak up the bacon flavor as it sits, so it is perfect to make ahead and take to a picnic or potluck event. Note, cooking the potatoes with the skins on prevents them from turning mushy when cubed.

Serves 8–10

2   pounds Russet potatoes
¾   cup cooked and crumbled
        bacon (about 8 slices)
½   cup sliced green onions
½   cup thinly sliced celery
½   cup sliced black olives
        (optional)
Sage Dressing (recipe follows)

Scrub the potatoes and cut them in half. Cover the potato halves with cold water in a large pot. Bring to a boil. Cook until potatoes are tender but not falling apart, about 20 minutes. Drain and cool until they are easy to handle. Peel and cut the potatoes into 1½-inch cubes.

Combine the cooked potatoes, bacon, green onions, celery, and olives (if using) in a large bowl and toss well with Sage Dressing until fully coated. Cover and chill for at least 1 hour, or overnight.

Serve chilled.

SAGE DRESSING

¼   cup white wine vinegar
1   teaspoon granulated sugar
1   teaspoon salt
1   teaspoon freshly ground black
        pepper
½   teaspoon rubbed sage
½   cup vegetable oil or light
        olive oil

In a small bowl, whisk together the vinegar, sugar, salt, pepper, and sage. Add the oil in a slow, steady stream, whisking constantly. Refrigerate until ready to use.

*Over-the-top bacon lover's tip:

Toss the cooked, cubed potatoes in 1 to 2 tablespoons Clarified Bacon Fat (page 22) before adding the remaining ingredients.

BACON BLT SANDWICH

Real bacon lovers don't settle for a simple BLT. This is our over-the-top version, with freshly made Bacon Mayonnaise on thick slices of crispy, smoked bacon with avocado, arugula leaves, and juicy slices of sweet heirloom tomato. Bacon mayonnaise is available commercially, but nothing compares to this version made with real bacon fat. We like a locally made rustic multi-grain bread, but you can substitute your favorite.

Makes 4 sandwiches

8   slices of artisan multi-grain bread, toasted
¼   cup Bacon Mayonnaise (recipe follows)
8   slices heirloom tomato
1   avocado, sliced
2   cups arugula, loosely packed
12 slices thick-cut bacon, cooked (page 12)

Spread the Bacon Mayonnaise liberally on the toast slices. Divide the tomato slices, avocado slices, and arugula evenly among four slices of bread. Top with bacon and the remaining pieces of toast. Serve immediately.

BACON MAYONNAISE

2   egg yolks
1   teaspoon Dijon mustard
1   teaspoon freshly squeezed lemon juice
¼   cup Clarified Bacon Fat, melted, but not hot (page 22)
¼   cup vegetable oil or light olive oil
¾   teaspoon salt
Freshly ground white pepper

Combine the egg yolks, mustard, and lemon juice in the bowl of a food processor, blender, or stand mixer. Combine the bacon fat and oil in a liquid measuring cup. With the machine running, gradually add the mixture, a few drops at a time, to the egg mixture. Gradually increase to a thin stream to form a fully emulsified mayonnaise. Season to taste with salt and pepper. Refrigerate until ready to use. Because of the bacon fat, the mayonnaise may harden more than usual when it is chilled. It can still be spread, or you can leave it at room temperature for 30 minutes to soften.

DECONSTRUCTED BLT

Like gazpacho, this soup is best when it is made with the freshest, most flavorful summer produce. All of the components of a classic BLT are in here, but the presentation is all new. The bread is part of the broth, the lettuce forms the cup, and the soup is garnished with "cookies"—delicate disks of crisp bacon made from pressed and molded slivers of sliced bacon.

Serves 6

1½   cups tomato juice
2   cups French bread, crust removed and cut into 1-inch cubes
12   medium tomatoes peeled, seeded, and chopped (about 7 cups)
1   English cucumber, peeled, seeded, and chopped (about 1 cup)
3   cloves garlic, chopped
½   cup chopped red bell pepper
½   cup chopped red onion
¼   cup chopped cilantro
2   tablespoon freshly squeezed lime juice
2   teaspoons salt
2   teaspoons smoked paprika
1   teaspoon ground cumin
¼   teaspoon freshly ground black pepper
1   cup extra virgin olive oil
6   Bibb lettuce leaves, washed and dried
Additional diced cucumber, for garnish
6   (3-inch) Bacon "Cookies" (recipe follows)

In a small bowl, combine tomato juice and bread cubes and let soak until the bread is very soft, about 30 minutes. Transfer the mixture to a blender and puree until smooth. Add the tomatoes, cucumber, garlic, bell pepper, onion, cilantro, lime juice, salt, paprika, cumin, and pepper. Blend to a very smooth puree. You may need to work in batches. With the mixer running on high speed, add the oil slowly, in a steady stream. Cover and refrigerate the gazpacho until it is well chilled, at least 1 hour.

Place a Bibb lettuce leaf in the center of six bowls. Ladle the chilled gazpacho over lettuce cups into the bowls, sprinkle with diced cucumber and garnish with a Bacon "Cookie." Serve immediately.

BACON "COOKIES"

Makes 6

6   slices bacon, sliced into ⅛-inch slivers

Preheat oven to 400°F. Line a baking sheet with parchment paper. Make "cookies" by packing one slice of slivered bacon, about 2 tablespoons, into a 3-inch pastry mold or biscuit cutter. Lift the mold off, leaving a round of compressed bacon slivers. Repeat with the remaining bacon. Bake until brown and crispy, about 15 minutes. Carefully remove bacon "cookies" from the tray with a spatula and transfer to paper towels to cool.

BROS, BEERS,
AND BRATS

Are you one of those people with a brother who considers brats and beer to be his "special" recipe? Maybe you are that brother? Even if you are an only child, this bacon-enriched, sauerkraut-simmered variation of the Midwestern classic is how good brats deserve to be done.

Serves 6

8	slices of bacon, chopped into 2-inch pieces (about 2 cups)
1	large onion, thinly sliced
1	(12-ounce) bottle of lager-style beer
4	cups sauerkraut, drained
2	tablespoons ketchup
1	teaspoon caraway seeds
1	teaspoon fennel seeds
1	teaspoon cracked black peppercorns
2	bay leaves
6	bratwurst sausages

Rye bread or hoagie rolls
Stone-ground or Dijon mustard

Heat a large, deep sauté pan or Dutch oven over medium heat. Cook the bacon until it is brown, but not completely crisp, about 5 minutes. Add the onion and cook until soft and golden, about 7 minutes. Deglaze the pan with half the beer, scraping gently to dissolve any brown bits. Stir in the sauerkraut, ketchup, caraway seeds, fennel seeds, peppercorns, and remaining beer.

Add the bay leaves. Bring the sauerkraut to a boil, then reduce the heat to medium-low.

Pierce each bratwurst on both sides with the tip of a knife. Nestle the sausages into the sauerkraut. Cover the pan and simmer for 20 to 25 minutes, turning the sausages and stirring the sauerkraut occasionally. At this point the sausages can be served as is, or if you prefer a crispier skin for your bratwurst continue as follows.

Position a rack in center of the oven and preheat the broiler.

Lift the cooked sausages from the sauerkraut and arrange them on a lightly-greased, foil-lined baking sheet. Roast until the edges of the sausages begin to brown, about 3 to 5 minutes per side.

Serve bratwurst with sauerkraut on rye bread or hoagie rolls slathered with mustard.

BLT SUSHI HAND ROLL WITH WASABI MAYO

Here is an unexpected, light, and gluten-free version of a BLT. I like using a lean slab bacon cut precisely into strips to give it a clean Japanese presentation. It's like SPAM sushi, but infinitely better.

Makes 10 sushi rolls

1½ cup short-grain sushi rice
1½ cups plus 2 tablespoons water
2   tablespoons rice vinegar
1   tablespoon mirin
1½ tablespoons granulated sugar
1   teaspoon kosher salt
10 ounces slab bacon
2   tablespoons Kewpie mayonnaise or Bacon Mayonnaise (page 84)
1   teaspoon premade wasabi paste
5   toasted nori sheets, cut in half to make 10 rectangles
1   tomato (preferably heirloom), sliced
1   avocado, sliced
4   ounces radish sprouts

Wash sushi rice thoroughly in cold water three to four times to remove excess starch. If using a rice cooker, follow the manufacturer's instructions for cooking sushi rice. If cooking on the stovetop, place the washed rice and 1½ cups plus 2 tablespoons of water in a saucepan with a tight-fitting lid. Allow rice to soak for 30 minutes. Bring to a boil over high heat. Turn the heat down to low and cook for 10 minutes, keeping rice covered. Remove from heat and allow to sit in the pan for an additional 10 minutes. Do not remove the lid.

Meanwhile, mix vinegar, mirin, sugar, and salt together in a small saucepan. Simmer over medium heat until sugar and salt dissolve. Remove from heat.

Spread cooked rice evenly onto a sheet pan and gently fold in vinegar mixture. Continue to gently fold rice for about 10 minutes until cooled. You can use a fan to help cool the rice down faster. Keep rice covered with a damp towel until ready to use. There may be leftover rice after assembling the sushi.

Cut bacon into thick strips measuring about ½ inch wide by 3 inches long. Cook bacon strips in a skillet over medium heat until browned and crisp, about 10 minutes, turning occasionally. Transfer to paper towel–lined plate.

In a small bowl, whisk together the mayonnaise and wasabi until well combined.

To assemble hand rolls, place a nori sheet horizontally on a work surface so the widest side is facing you. Using moistened fingers, place a golf ball–size portion of rice on the left side of the nori and gently spread the rice to cover about a third of the nori sheet. Spread a scant ½ teaspoon of wasabi mayonnaise over the rice. Top with one or two tomato slices, one or two avocado slices, one or two pieces of bacon, and a small handful of radish sprouts. Don't go overboard with the fillings or it will be too difficult to roll the sushi.

Starting at the bottom left corner, roll the nori over the rice and fillings, creating a cone shape. Adhere the outside corner of the hand roll with a dab of water to seal the end shut. Serve immediately.

BACON-WRAPPED, BACON-WRAPPED JALAPEÑO HOT DOGS

I was raised in Chicago where they make the perfect hot dog with spicy peppers and celery salt. But now I live in Seattle where they make the perfect hot dog with cream cheese. But in southern California, where my sister lives, they also make the perfect hot dog wrapped in bacon. I just can't decide so I'll have all three at the same time!

Makes 4 hot dogs

4   beef hot dogs
12   slices thin-cut bacon, uncooked
4   jalapeño peppers
2   ounces cream cheese, softened
2   ounces freshly shredded sharp Cheddar (about 1 cup loosely packed)
4   hot dog buns
Celery salt, for garnish

Preheat a gas or charcoal grill to 400°F.

Wrap each hot dog with one slice of bacon in a spiral pattern, tucking the bacon ends under the spiral to secure. Depending on the length of the hot dogs, the bacon may not cover the entire hot dog. Keep in the refrigerator while you prepare the rest of the bacon.

Take the remaining eight slices of bacon and lay them flat on a paper towel–lined, microwave-safe plate. Cover with an additional paper towel. You may need to work in batches. Par-cook in the microwave for 2 minutes. Set aside and allow to cool.

Meanwhile, cut the jalapeños in half lengthwise and remove the seeds and membrane. Keep the stems attached as this will help keep the filling in during grilling.

In a food processor, process cream cheese until smooth. Add shredded cheddar and pulse until fully combined.

Fill each cavity of the jalapeños with about 1 tablespoon of cream cheese filling. Wrap completely with par-cooked bacon slices. Tuck the bacon ends in or secure with a toothpick soaked in water if necessary. Refrigerate bacon-wrapped jalapeños for 10 minutes.

Grill bacon-wrapped hot dogs for 6 to 8 minutes, rotating every 1 to 2 minutes to cook the bacon on all sides.

Place jalapeños on the grill, filling side down, and grill for 1½ minutes. Flip jalapeños over and grill for 2 minutes. Move jalapeños to the warming rack, if available, or to a low heat section of the grill while the hot dogs finish cooking.

Place grilled hot dogs in warm hot dog buns and sprinkle with celery salt. Top with grilled jalapeños, remove the stems and toothpicks (if using) before serving.

BACON
BUTTERNUT
SQUASH SOUP

This is a velvety, comforting soup garnished with bacon, crispy fried sage leaves and roasted, salted pumpkin seeds. It is perfect for fall or winter. Serve it in tiny bowls as a first course, or in bigger portions as an entrée.

Serves 4–6

6	slices bacon, coarsely chopped (about 1½ cups)
3	carrots, chopped (about 1½ cups)
2	shallots, minced
2	cloves garlic, minced
1	teaspoon salt
½	teaspoon freshly ground black pepper
1	tablespoon chopped fresh sage
2	teaspoons chopped fresh thyme
1	bay leaf
6	cups 1-inch cubes of fresh or frozen butternut squash (about 1½ pounds)
4	cups chicken or vegetable stock
1	teaspoon apple cider vinegar
¼	teaspoon grated nutmeg
¼	cup roasted, salted pepitas (pumpkin seeds)

Fried Sage Leaves (recipe follows)

Cook the bacon in a large soup pot over medium heat until almost crisp, about 6 minutes. Transfer to paper towels, reserving rendered bacon fat in the pot.

Cook the carrots, shallots, and garlic in the reserved bacon fat until soft and golden, about 5 minutes. Stir in the salt and pepper. Add the chopped herbs, bay leaf, squash cubes, stock, and half of the cooked bacon to the soup pot. Bring the soup to a boil, then reduce the heat to medium-low and simmer, stirring occasionally, until the squash is tender, 20 to 25 minutes. Remove and discard the bay leaf.

Blend the soup to a smooth puree with an immersion blender or in batches in a traditional blender. Season with vinegar and nutmeg. Keep the soup warm until it is ready to serve.

Ladle the soup into warm bowls and garnish with reserved bacon, pepitas, and Fried Sage Leaves.

FRIED SAGE LEAVES

Vegetable oil, for deep-frying
10–12 fresh sage leaves

Heat the oil in a saucepan to 350°F. Deep-fry the sage leaves until they are crisp, about 10 seconds. Transfer to paper towels.

BLT MAC AND CHEESE

Bacon and melted cheese is a magical pairing, but many bacon mac and cheese recipes seem intensely salty or cloying. BLT mac and cheese...now that's a whole different story! Tomatoes and fresh basil brighten up the dish for a much better balance. The dish is still very rich, which is why we include the "L" as a simple, crisp salad served alongside. To keep the pasta from absorbing too much liquid, we assemble the casserole at the last minute and brown it in a hot oven.

Serves 6

½   pound cellantani or similar curly pasta
6   slices bacon, coarsely chopped (about 1½ cup)
2   leeks, halved lengthwise and sliced, white and light green parts only (about 1½ cup)
2   cloves garlic, chopped
¼   teaspoon red pepper flakes
¾   cup half-and-half
¼   cup tomato sauce
1   cup mascarpone (8 ounces)
1   cup shredded Parmesan
Salt
Freshly ground black pepper
1   cup cherry tomatoes, halved
1   cup packed, chopped basil leaves
¼   cup dry bread crumbs
6–8 cups baby arugula or baby spinach, washed and dried
Sage Dressing (page 81) made with basil, or substitute your favorite commercial vinaigrette

Preheat oven to 450°F. Lightly grease a deep (9-by-13-inch) casserole or baking dish.

Bring a large pot of salted water to a boil. Add the pasta and cook, according to package directions, until al dente. Drain.

Cook the bacon in a large skillet over medium heat until just starting to crisp, about 6 minutes. Add the leeks and cook until they are softened, 2 to 3 minutes. Add the garlic and pepper flakes and cook for 1 minute more. Stir in the half-and-half and tomato sauce until well combined. Add the mascarpone, and simmer, stirring constantly until it is melted. Remove the pan from the heat, add ¾ cup of the Parmesan and season to taste with salt and pepper.

Combine the sauce, cooked

pasta, cherry tomatoes, and basil and gently toss to coat. Transfer to the prepared casserole or baking dish and sprinkle with the bread crumbs and remaining ¼ cup of Parmesan. Bake until bubbling at the edges and is browned on top, about 15 minutes.

In a large bowl, toss the arugula or spinach with vinaigrette. Serve the greens alongside warm portions of pasta.

STEAMED MUSSELS WITH TOMATO AND FENNEL

Cooking mussels with tomatoes and fennel in a light bacon broth creates a dish reminiscent of sea breezes. You'll need a whole loaf of crusty bread to sop up all the precious broth.

Serves 4

2   pounds fresh mussels
6   slices bacon, coarsely chopped
     (about 1½ cups)
1   large shallot, minced (about ⅓ cup)
4   cloves garlic, minced
1½   cups sliced fennel bulb
2   cups dry white wine, such as a
     Sauvignon Blanc
½   cup (1 stick) butter, melted
1   (28-ounce) can whole tomatoes
½   cup packed, chopped basil leaves
3   tablespoons chopped flat-leaf
     parsley
Artisan bread or baguette

Scrub and de-beard the mussels.

Cook the bacon in a large stock pot over medium heat until it is almost crisp, about 6 minutes. Add the shallots, garlic, and fennel and cook for 1 minute. Add the mussels to the pot along with the wine and butter. Lightly crush the tomatoes by hand and add them to the pot with the juices. Cover and cook, stirring occasionally, until all of the mussels have opened, 7 to 10 minutes. Remove from heat and stir in the basil and parsley.

Ladle the mussels and broth into bowls and serve hot with plenty of bread for dipping in the broth.

GRAPE AND GORGONZOLA PIZZETTAS

Individual "pizzettas" like these are the perfect size for a light lunch, starter, a cocktail nosh, or a late night snack. Use your favorite pizza dough recipe or any good-quality commercially prepared pizza dough.

Makes 4 (6-inch) individual pizzas

1	(1-pound) package prepared pizza dough
3	cups red seedless grapes, rinsed and stemmed
1	large red onion, thinly sliced (about 2 cups)
¼	cup olive oil, divided
¾	teaspoon salt, divided
1	cup ricotta
1	tablespoon Italian seasoning
1	teaspoon chopped garlic
¼	teaspoon freshly ground black pepper
1	cup crumbled Gorgonzola (8 ounces)
8	slices thick-cut, peppered bacon, par-cooked (page 12)

If the pizza dough is cold, let it sit at room temperature while you prepare the toppings.

If you have a pizza stone, put it in the cold oven. If you do not have a pizza stone, the pizzettas can be baked on a baking sheet. Preheat oven to 425°F.

Toss the grapes and onions with about 3 tablespoons of olive oil and ½ teaspoon of salt. Spread them in a single layer on a baking sheet. Roast until the grapes are wrinkled and the onions are soft, about 25 minutes.

In a medium bowl, mix together the ricotta, Italian seasoning, garlic, pepper, the remaining 1 tablespoon of olive oil, and ¼ teaspoon of salt.

Divide the pizza dough into four equal pieces.

On a lightly floured surface or floured pizza peel, roll out the dough pieces into 6-inch rounds. Spread a quarter of the ricotta mixture onto each pizza, leaving ½ inch of space around the edges. Cover each pizza evenly with the grape and onion mixture and crumbled Gorgonzola. Break two slices of bacon onto each pizza. Bake pizzettas on the preheated pizza stone or on lightly oiled baking sheets until the crust is golden brown, 10 to 12 minutes.

Serve hot.

DUSK

DUSK

TERIYAKI SALMON SKEWERS WITH BACON AND PINEAPPLE

One skewer has all the flavors and textures you can imagine—salty, sweet, savory, tangy, silky, crisp, and fresh. Once you learn how simple it is to throw together a perfect teriyaki sauce, you will never go back to the commercial bottles. Mirin is a very mild, sweet Japanese rice wine. Use only top-quality salmon for the best results. Weaving the bacon and assorted ingredients together on the skewer looks nice, but it also secures the bacon on the skewer more solidly and helps to distribute the flavor and fat evenly.

Makes 20 skewers

½   cup soy sauce
2   tablespoons mirin
2   tablespoons rice wine vinegar
2   tablespoons light brown sugar
1   tablespoon minced ginger
1½ pounds salmon fillet, skin and
     pin bones removed, cut into
     1-inch cubes
Salt
1   fresh pineapple, peeled, cored,
     and cut into 2-inch cubes
     (about 5 cups)
10   slices thick-cut bacon, cut in
     half crosswise, par-cooked
     (page 12)
20   bamboo skewers

Combine the soy sauce, mirin, vinegar, brown sugar, and ginger in a small saucepan. Bring to a boil over high heat, then simmer over medium-low heat until the sauce has reduced by half, about 10 minutes. Pour half of the sauce into a small serving dish.

Preheat oven to 400°F

Line a baking sheet with foil and place a wire rack on top. Season the salmon cubes well with salt. Weave a slice of bacon onto each bamboo skewer, followed by pineapple and salmon cubes, finishing with a cube of salmon. Place the skewer on the rack and repeat with the remaining ingredients and skewers.

Brush each skewer with teriyaki sauce. Bake the glazed skewers until the bacon is crisp and the salmon is just cooked through, 5 to 7 minutes.

Serve warm with the reserved bowl of teriyaki sauce and toasted sesame seeds (optional) alongside.

BACON-WRAPPED SCALLOPS WITH PAPAYA PINEAPPLE GLAZE

Bacon-wrapped scallops are wildly popular, and with good reason. This version uses good quality, plump sea scallops and adds a hint of the tropics with reduced papaya nectar and pineapple juice. Served on a bed of wild rice, this is a wonderfully elegant dish for entertaining. Papaya nectar is available at gourmet supermarkets.

Serves 4

12   sea scallops
1   cup papaya nectar, such as Goya brand
½   cup pineapple juice
2   tablespoons freshly squeezed lime juice
1   teaspoon grated ginger
12   slices thin-cut bacon, par-cooked (page 12)
Salt
Freshly ground black pepper
4   tablespoons (½ stick) butter
Cooked wild rice, for serving

Rinse and dry the scallops. Remove and discard the small, tough muscle from the sides of the scallops if they haven't already been removed. Refrigerate until ready to use.

Combine the papaya nectar, pineapple juice, lime juice, and ginger in a saucepan. Bring to a boil on high and then reduce the heat to medium. Simmer until it is reduced to a syrupy glaze, about 20 minutes.

Season the scallops with salt and pepper. Wrap one piece of bacon around each scallop, securing overlapping edges with toothpicks. Melt butter in a large skillet over medium-high heat. Sear scallops turning & basting with glaze every two minutes until they are just cooked and the bacon is crisp, 5 to 7 minutes.

Remove the toothpicks and serve the scallops hot with wild rice and the remaining glaze alongside.

BRUSSELS SPROUTS WITH LEMON AND HONEY

This side dish goes well with any kind of meat, but is especially nice with holiday dishes like roast turkey or prime rib. Look for fresh Brussels sprouts still on the stalk, you will find them to be less bitter than loose sprouts.

Serves 4

1	pound Brussels sprouts, trimmed
4	slices thick-cut bacon, coarsely chopped (about 1 cup)
1	cup thinly sliced, red onion (about ½ an onion)
1	tablespoons olive oil
¼	cup honey
1	tablespoon lemon zest

Salt
Freshly ground black pepper

Bring a large pot of salted water to a boil. Set up an ice bath alongside.

Boil the Brussels sprouts until they are almost tender, about 5 minutes. Drain the sprouts and then immediately plunge them in the ice bath to stop the cooking. Drain well. Pat dry, and cut each sprout in half, lengthwise.

Cook the bacon in a large skillet over medium heat until just starting to crisp, about 6 minutes. Add the onions and continue to cook until bacon is crisp and onions are tender, about 2 minutes longer. Transfer to a bowl and cover with foil to keep warm.

Add the olive oil to the same skillet the bacon and onions were cooked in and turn the heat up to medium-high. Add the Brussels sprouts and cook until the sprouts are seared brown on the edges, 4 to 5 minutes. Return the bacon and onions to the skillet with the Brussels sprouts. Add the honey and lemon. Turn off the heat and stir until the honey is melted and the sprouts are evenly glazed, about 1 minute. Season to taste with salt and pepper.

Serve immediately.

PASTA ALLA CARBONARA

This is a great "go-to" dish when unexpected guests stop by because so many of the ingredients are usually on hand. Fresh pasta is always best, but if dried pasta is the only option, it works too. More wine, anyone?

Serves 4

1   tablespoon olive oil
4   slices bacon, diced (about ¾ cup)
1   cup shredded Parmigiano-Reggiano
2   large eggs
2   large egg yolks
½   cup heavy cream
½   teaspoon salt
½   teaspoon freshly ground black pepper
10   ounces fresh linguine
1   cup frozen peas
Additional Parmigiano-Reggiano, for serving

Bring a large pot of salted water to a boil.

Heat the oil in a large skillet over medium heat. Add the bacon and cook until it is almost crisp, about 6 minutes. Reduce the heat to low and stir now and then while you prepare the remaining ingredients.

In a medium bowl, whisk together the cheese, eggs, egg yolks, cream, salt, and pepper.

Cook the pasta al dente, following the packaging cooking instructions. When there is 1 minute remaining on the pasta, add the peas. Drain the pasta and peas, reserving ¼ cup of the pasta cooking water. Add the pasta, peas, and reserved liquid to the skillet with the bacon. Toss gently to combine. Add the cheese and egg mixture and toss gently. Cook until the pasta is warm and thoroughly coated in the sauce, about 2 minutes.

Serve immediately with additional Parmigiano-Reggiano and black pepper alongside.

MISO BLACK COD WITH BACON FRIED RICE

This miso-marinated cod, inspired by Nobu Matsuhisa, is superb. Especially when served along with Bacon Fried Rice, making it a well-rounded dish with the perfect balance of sweet, salty, and umami.

Serves 4

4 (6-ounce) fillets black cod, skin removed
¼ cup sake
¼ cup mirin
¼ cup superfine sugar
½ cup white miso paste

In a small saucepan over high heat, bring sake and mirin to a boil. Boil for 30 seconds. Add the sugar and stir to dissolve. Turn the heat down to low and add miso paste. Stir constantly until smooth. The marinade will be thick. Remove from heat and cool to room temperature.

Place black cod fillets in a gallon-size resealable bag and pour in miso marinade. Make sure each fillet is covered in marinade, seal the bag, and refrigerate for 24 to 48 hours.

Set oven rack to the middle position and set the broiler to high. Line a sheet pan with non-stick foil, and remove black cod from marinade and place on sheet pan, at least 2 inches apart. Broil for 8 to 10 minutes. The fish will flake and separate slightly, making it easier to remove the bones before serving.

(Note: Making the Bacon Fried Rice takes about 20 minutes so plan accordingly.)

BACON FRIED RICE

1½ cups slab bacon, diced (about ½ pound)
3 cups cooked white rice, chilled
6 ounces shiitake mushrooms, sliced and stems removed
4 scallions, sliced, white parts and green parts separated
2 tablespoons vegetable oil
2 tablespoons soy sauce
1 teaspoon minced ginger
1 teaspoon toasted sesame seeds, plus more for garnish

In a large skillet over medium heat, add diced bacon. Cook bacon until crisp, about 10 minutes. Remove bacon with a slotted spoon and set aside, reserving rendered fat in the pan. Add the white parts of the scallions and cook for 30 seconds. Add the sliced shiitake mushrooms and cook until softened, about 4 minutes, stirring often. Add minced ginger and stir to just combine, do not overcook. Remove mushrooms and ginger with a slotted spoon and set aside. Add 2 tablespoons oil to the skillet. Once the oil is heated, add rice and cook for 3 minutes, stirring frequently. Add soy sauce and cook for an additional minute, stirring constantly. Add the green parts of the scallions, the sesame seeds, the mushroom mixture, and all but ⅓ cup of the cooked bacon. Stir to combine.

Divide rice among four plates, top with miso cod fillets, and garnish with remaining cooked bacon and sesame seeds. Serve immediately.

FRANCE'S FAVORITE LENTILS

Lentils may not be the first thing that comes to mind when the cuisine of France is discussed, but the French do prepare them brilliantly. French green lentils, also known as Puy lentils, are more plump and meaty than the common brown or orange varieties. This hearty warm dish is also delicious served cold as a salad the next day. Peeling pearl onions can be labor intensive so you can do them one day ahead and store in the refrigerator.

Serves 4

1   (6-ounce) package white pearl onions (about 15 onions)
6   slices bacon, coarsely chopped (about 1½ cups)
1   large carrot, sliced (about ½ cup)
4   cloves garlic, thinly sliced
2   teaspoons salt
½   teaspoon freshly ground black pepper
1   cup French green lentils, rinsed
4   cups water
5   fresh thyme sprigs
1   bay leaf
3   tablespoons unsalted butter
1   tablespoon Dijon mustard
Artisan bread or toasted baguette slices, for serving

To peel the pearl onions, bring a pot of water to boil and arrange an ice bath alongside. Blanch the onions in the water for 1 minute. Scoop out of the boiling water and plunge into the waiting ice bath to stop the cooking. Drain the onions and use your fingers to pop the onions from their loosened skins.

Cook the bacon in a large skillet over medium heat until almost crisp, about 5 minutes. Add the peeled onions and cook for 5 minutes more. Add the carrots, garlic, salt, and pepper and cook until the vegetables are soft and the onions are slightly caramelized, about 5 minutes. Stir in the lentils, water, thyme sprigs, and bay leaf. Bring the lentils to a boil and then reduce the heat to low and simmer, uncovered, until the lentils are tender and most of the liquid has been absorbed, 20 to 30 minutes.

Add the butter and mustard just before serving. Stir until the butter is melted and the ingredients are evenly combined.

Serve warm with bread or toasted baguette slices.

KOREAN-STYLE HANGOVER STEW

This spicy stew is treasured as a remedy for the previous night's excesses. Kimchi is the answer for pretty much all that ails you, according to many Korean grandmothers. This spicy, hearty stew will get you back on your feet in no time. Cabbage kimchi, firm tofu, and mirin are widely available. You may have to go to a Korean market for kochujang, a marvelous fermented chili paste. There is no real substitute, so it is worth seeking out. Kochukaru is a fine red chili powder that is flavorful without being too fiery. If you're head is pounding so hard you can't leave the house, you can use other chili pastes and unseasoned chili powders. You will need to adjust the quantity.

Heat the sesame oil in a large soup pot over medium heat. Add the bacon and onion and cook until the onions are softened and the bacon is browned but not crisp, about 5 minutes. Stir in the garlic and ginger and cook for 1 minute more. Add the chili paste and chili powder and stir to combine. Add the chopped kimchi with juices and water.

Bring the soup to a boil and then reduce the heat to low. Add the tofu and simmer gently for 20 to 30 minutes to deepen the flavors. Season with mirin and soy sauce.

Top with green onions and serve hot with white rice.

Serves 4

1   tablespoon sesame oil
6   slices thick-cut bacon, cut into 2-inch pieces (about 1½ cups)
1   onion, thinly sliced (about 2 cups)
2   cloves garlic, minced
1   tablespoon minced ginger
1   tablespoon kochujang, Korean fermented red chili paste
1   tablespoon kochukaru, fine Korean red chili powder
2   cups kimchi with juices, chopped
4   cups water
1   (14-ounce) carton firm tofu, drained and cubed
¼   cup mirin
1   tablespoon soy sauce
1   cup sliced green onions (about 1 bunch)
3   cups cooked white rice

CRAB AND CORN CHOWDER

Rich, complex, and easy to make for a weeknight supper. If you can't find fresh Dungeness crab meat, you may substitute a variety that is fresh in your area.

Serves 4–6

6   slices thick-cut bacon, coarsely chopped (about 1½ cups)
1   onion, chopped (about 1½ cups)
2   celery ribs, chopped (about ½ cup)
2   medium carrots, chopped (about ½ cup)
1   teaspoon salt
½   teaspoon freshly ground black pepper
1   red bell pepper, chopped (about 1 cup)
2   cloves garlic, minced
2   teaspoons dried thyme
2   tablespoons all-purpose flour
½   cup dry white wine
4   cups chicken or fish stock
1   bay leaf
8   ounces baby red potatoes or new potatoes, quartered
1   pound Dungeness crab meat, picked clean of any shells
2   cups fresh or frozen sweet corn kernels
½   cup heavy cream
2   teaspoons chopped fresh parsley
¼   teaspoon cayenne pepper
Artisan bread or oyster crackers, for serving

Cook the bacon in a large soup pot over medium heat until crisp, about 8 minutes. Transfer to paper towels, reserving rendered bacon fat in the pot.

Cook the onion, celery, carrot, salt, and black pepper in the bacon fat until the onions are soft and translucent, about 5 minutes. Add the red bell pepper, garlic, and thyme and cook for another 2 minutes. Stir in the flour, making sure that the vegetables are evenly coated. Add the wine and allow it to simmer and reduce slightly. Add 4 cups of stock, bay leaf, and the potatoes. Bring the soup to a boil over high heat, reduce the temperature to medium-low and simmer uncovered, for about 20 minutes. Add the crab and corn and simmer gently until the potatoes and corn are tender, about 5 additional minutes.

Finish with the cream and keep warm until ready to serve.

Just before serving, stir in the parsley and cayenne pepper. Ladle the soup into bowls and top with reserved crumbled bacon. Serve bowls of soup with artisan bread or oyster crackers.

BACON-WRAPPED BEEF TENDERLOINS WITH POMEGRANATE GLAZE

As with bacon, if you are going to indulge in something, it only makes sense to buy the very best. Go to your local butcher and buy steaks that will make you proud. You might want to make a little extra sauce to keep your guests from licking their plates at such a nice dinner.

Serves 4

4   beef tenderloin steaks (4–6 ounces each)
Salt
Coarsely ground black pepper
4   slices thick-cut, peppered bacon
2   tablespoons olive oil
Pomegranate Glaze (recipe follows)

Preheat oven to 450°F.

Sprinkle each steak very generously with salt and pepper. Wrap each steak with one slice of bacon, securing the ends with a toothpick.

Heat the olive oil in a large skillet, preferably cast-iron, over high heat. Sear the steaks to a nice brown, about 2 minutes on each side. Using a pair of tongs, carefully roll the steaks on their sides to quickly sear the bacon all the way around. Transfer the skillet to the oven and cook, flipping the steaks once halfway through cooking, until the steaks are done to your liking and the bacon is just cooked through, 5 to 7 minutes for medium-rare.

Remove and discard the toothpicks.

Serve the steaks hot, drizzled with Pomegranate Glaze.

POMEGRANATE GLAZE

1   cup pomegranate juice
½   cup balsamic vinegar
¼   cup light brown sugar
4   teaspoons chopped fresh rosemary
Salt

Combine the pomegranate juice, vinegar, sugar, and rosemary. Bring to a boil over high heat, then simmer over medium heat until reduced by half, about 15 to 18 minutes. Season to taste with salt.

*Over-the-top bacon lover's tip:

Brush steaks with a little melted Clarified Bacon Fat (page 22) before seasoning.

CHICKEN NORMANDY, OF SORTS

Normandy, like the Pacific Northwest, is famed for their apple orchards. Consider this variation of a classic recipe next time you feel yourself trapped in a chicken breast rut. It's quick to prepare and especially warming on a chilly autumn evening when served with mashed potatoes.

Serves 4

4	slices bacon, coarsely chopped (about 1 cup)
4	skin-on, boneless chicken breasts
	Salt
	Freshly ground black pepper
¼	cup all-purpose flour
1	cup thinly sliced onions (about half a small onion)
½	cup dry sherry
1	cup apple cider
½	cup heavy cream
1	crisp red apple, sliced (about 2 cups)
1	tablespoon chopped fresh thyme

Cook the bacon in a large skillet over medium heat until crisp, about 8 minutes. Transfer to paper towels, reserving rendered bacon fat in the skillet. Season the chicken on all sides with salt and pepper. Dredge the chicken with flour, shaking to remove the excess. Cook the chicken in the reserved bacon fat over medium heat until it is golden brown and nearly cooked through, about 6 minutes per side. Remove the chicken from the skillet and keep it warm while you prepare the sauce.

Cook the onions in the skillet until they are soft and translucent, about 6 minutes. Add the sherry and simmer to reduce it slightly. Add the cider and simmer until reduced by half, about 5 minutes. Add the apples, thyme, and cooked bacon to the sauce and stir to combine. Stir in the cream and add the chicken breasts with any juices that may have collected to the skillet. Simmer until the chicken is fully cooked, about 5 additional minutes.

Serve hot.

WRAPPED-UP, GLAZED-UP PORK TENDERLOIN

Without question, this is one of the most popular recipes in the whole book. The pork is juicy, tender, and flavorful and the easy-to-make glaze tastes like it took all day to make. This recipe makes extra rub for another use.

Serves 4

1   (1-pound) pork tenderloin
2   tablespoons light brown sugar
1   tablespoon paprika
1   tablespoon freshly ground black pepper
1   tablespoon coarse salt
2   teaspoons chili powder
¼   teaspoon cayenne pepper
6   slices thin-cut, applewood smoked bacon
2   tablespoons olive oil
1   (13-ounce) jar apricot preserves
1   (4-ounce) jar sweet-hot mustard, such as Inglehoffer brand
1   tablespoon chopped fresh rosemary

Preheat oven to 350°F.

Trim the pork of excess fat and membrane.

In a small bowl, combine the brown sugar, paprika, black pepper, salt, chili powder, and cayenne. Rub the pork generously with the spice mixture. Store any extra spice rub in an airtight container for another use.

Wrap the pork in strips of bacon, overlapping the pieces slightly and tucking the ends underneath to hold them in place.

Heat the oil in a roasting pan or a large skillet over medium-high heat. Sear the pork until it is brown on all sides, about 8 minutes total. Transfer the pan to the oven and bake the tenderloin until the core temperature reaches 155°F, about 15 minutes.

While the pork is cooking, whisk together the apricot preserves and mustard in a small saucepan. Warm the mixture over medium-low heat until it begins to bubble, about 5 minutes. Remove the pan from the heat and stir in the rosemary. A few minutes before the pork is ready to come out of the oven, spoon a few tablespoons of glaze evenly over the meat. Continue cooking just to set the glaze.

Serve hot slices of the pork with the remaining glaze alongside.

ONION AND BACON JAM

In Seattle, the buzz about Bacon Jam started when a local food truck, Skillet, started slathering it on their fabulous burgers and hot sandwiches. Jars of Skillet's Original Bacon Jam are now available online, but inspired chefs may prefer to make their own version. This is our favorite, with roasted garlic and shallots and a hint of black coffee. Use a spoonful with eggs, slather it on a grilled cheese sandwich, or put a delicate dollop on a canapé. The possibilities are endless.

Makes about 2½ cups

5   cloves garlic, unpeeled
2   shallots, unpeeled
2   tablespoons extra virgin olive oil
1   pound bacon, coarsely chopped (about 3 cups)
1   pound red onions, sliced (about 3 cups)
3   tablespoons light brown sugar
3   tablespoons maple syrup
1   teaspoon paprika
1   teaspoon ground cumin
1   teaspoon ground coriander
1   cup coffee
¼   cup sherry vinegar
1   teaspoon salt
1   teaspoon freshly ground black pepper

Preheat oven to 400°F.

Cut the garlic cloves and shallots in half, exposing the flesh but leaving the skins on. Place them on a double piece of foil and drizzle with the olive oil, tossing to coat. Seal the foil into a pouch and bake until the garlic and shallots are soft, about 30 minutes. Cool slightly until easy to handle, and remove the skins.

While the garlic and shallots are roasting, cook the bacon in a large Dutch oven or saucepan over medium heat until crisp, working in batches if needed, about 8 minutes per batch. Transfer to paper towels, reserving rendered bacon fat in the pan.

Pour out all but ¼ cup of the bacon fat. Save any extra fat for Clarified Bacon Fat (page 22). Add the sliced onions and cook, stirring occasionally, until the onions are soft, 10 to 12 minutes. Add the roasted garlic and shallots, mashing them a bit with the back of a spoon.

Return the bacon to the pot and stir in the remaining ingredients. Reduce the heat to low and simmer, partially covered, until the mixture becomes a deep, rich color and jam-like texture, about 2 hours. If the mixture begins to dry out before it is dark and soft, add a few tablespoons of water and stir often to prevent the jam from burning.

Transfer jam to the bowl of a food processor and pulse until the jam is roughly chopped and more spreadable.

Serve warm or store refrigerated in an airtight container for up to 2 weeks.

BUCATINI ALL'AMATRICIANA

Bucatini is a long pasta with a very thin hole in the center, so it is kind of like chewy spaghetti tubes. Sauce amatriciana is one of the oldest Italian tomato sauces. It is traditionally made with guanciale, or smoked pork cheek, but bacon has become a more common ingredient. Serve the pasta with plenty of shredded Pecorino-Romano, a loaf of crusty bread, and a good bottle of red wine.

Serves 4

1   tablespoon extra virgin olive oil
4   slices thick-cut bacon, coarsely chopped (about 1 cup)
1   small onion, finely minced (about 1 cup)
3   cloves garlic, sliced
¼   cup white wine
1   (28-ounce) can whole tomatoes with juices
2   tablespoons balsamic vinegar
½   teaspoon red chili flakes
½   teaspoon salt
¼   teaspoon freshly ground black pepper
1   pound bucatini pasta, or substitute spaghetti
⅓   cup shredded Pecorino-Romano
Additional Pecorino-Romano, for serving

Heat the oil in a large skillet over medium heat. Add the bacon and cook until it is just beginning to crisp, about 6 minutes. Add the onion and garlic, and cook until the onion is transparent, about 3 minutes. Add the wine and simmer to reduce, about 2 minutes longer. Add the tomatoes and vinegar. Crush the tomatoes with a spoon as they soften. Simmer until the sauce comes together, about 10 minutes. Season with chili flakes, salt, and pepper. Keep sauce warm over low heat while you cook the pasta.

Bring a large pot of salted water to a boil. Cook the pasta al dente, following the packaging cooking instructions. Drain well, reserving ¼ cup of pasta cooking water.

Add the pasta and reserved liquid to the sauce and return the skillet to medium heat. Toss the pasta gently until it is well coated and heated through, about 5 minutes. Fold in the cheese.

Serve the pasta hot with additional Pecorino-Romano alongside.

DARK

DARK

BACON MANHATTAN

Bacon-infused bourbon adds a gentle, savory perfume to this classic cocktail.

Makes 1 cocktail

2–3 dashes bitters
1½ ounces Bacon-Infused Bourbon (recipe follows)
½ ounce dry vermouth
¼ ounce sweet vermouth
1 maraschino or brandied cherry
1 twist of orange rind
1 strip of crisp, cooked bacon or Candied Bacon (page 170), for garnish

Swirl 2 to 3 dashes of bitters in a chilled martini glass. Fill a cocktail shaker with large ice cubes and add the bourbon and vermouths. Shake vigorously. Strain the cocktail into the prepared martini glass and garnish with the cherry, orange rind, and bacon. Serve immediately.

BACON-INFUSED BOURBON

This technique can be used to add a scent of bacon to many different liquids or liquors.

Makes 12 ounces of infused bourbon

12 ounces bourbon
2 ounces clarified bacon fat, melted

Combine the bourbon and bacon fat in a quart-size Mason jar. Seal with a tightly fitting lid and shake vigorously. Leave the bourbon to infuse at room temperature for 5 to 8 hours. Put the jar in the freezer and freeze until all of the bacon fat has solidified at the surface of the bourbon, about 1 hour. Scoop off and discard the bacon fat and strain the bourbon through a fine mesh sieve lined with two coffee filters. Store the bacon-infused bourbon at room temperature for up to 2 weeks, or in the refrigerator for up to 6 months.

CLAMS CASINO

No good cocktail or patio party of the 1950s would have been complete without a piping hot tray of Clams Casino. We think it is a tradition that should be revived, and improved upon. Use only fresh, live clams.

Makes 24 clams

Rock salt or kosher salt, as needed for baking
24 hard-shell clams, such as Manila or Butter clams, scrubbed clean
2   tablespoons olive oil
3   slices bacon, finely chopped (about ½ cup)
1   red bell pepper, minced (about 1 cup)
1   large shallot, minced (about ⅓ cup)
2   cloves garlic, minced
½   teaspoon dried oregano
¼   cup dry white wine
Zest and juice of 1 lemon
¼   cup shredded Parmesan, divided
Salt
Freshly ground black pepper

Cover a baking sheet with a thick, even layer of rock salt or kosher salt.

Shuck the clams, wearing a shucking glove for safety. Hold a clam securely while you insert a shucking knife between the shells. Pry the shells apart, and sever the adductor muscle connecting the shells. Discard the top shell. Loosen the clam meat and the muscle in the lower shell. Nestle the shucked clams in the prepared salt tray. Cover and refrigerate the shucked clams while you prepare the remaining ingredients.

Heat the oil in a large skillet over medium heat. Cook the bacon until it is crisp, about 8 minutes. Transfer to paper towels, reserving rendered bacon fat in the skillet. Cook the bell pepper, shallot, garlic, and oregano in the remaining bacon fat until the shallots are tender and translucent, about 5 minutes. Add the wine and the lemon juice and simmer until the liquid has almost completely evaporated. Transfer the mixture to a bowl and cool slightly.

Stir the reserved bacon, 2 tablespoons of Parmesan, and the lemon zest into the cooled vegetable mixture. Season with salt and pepper to taste.

Preheat the oven to 500°F.

Spoon 1 to 2 teaspoons of the bacon and vegetable mixture onto each clam, mounding the topping slightly. Sprinkle with the remaining Parmesan cheese. Bake until the clams are cooked through and the topping is golden, about 10 minutes.

Serve immediately.

BACON-WRAPPED STUFFED DATES

We all could use a really hot date now and then, right? Make these ahead of time and pop them in the oven when your guests arrive. Medjool dates are particularly large, moist, and meaty. The vinegar and orange juice adds a tangy balance to the sweet and salty flavors.

Makes 20 dates

20   pitted Medjool dates
½   cup crumbled blue cheese
10   slices bacon, cut in half crosswise, par-cooked (page 12)
½   cup balsamic vinegar
Zest and juice of 1 orange

Preheat oven to 450°F.

Line a baking sheet with parchment paper.

With a paring knife, make a slit in the center of each date. Carefully stuff each date with 1 teaspoon of blue cheese crumbles and wrap with bacon, securing the ends with a toothpick. Place the wrapped dates on the prepared tray and bake for 5 minutes. Flip the dates and bake for an additional 5 minutes, or until the bacon is crisp and the blue cheese begins to ooze.

While dates are baking, combine the vinegar, orange zest, and orange juice in a small saucepan. Bring the mixture to a boil over high heat and then reduce the heat to medium-high and simmer until the mixture has reduced to a thick, syrupy glaze, about 10 minutes. Strain the glaze through a fine-mesh strainer.

Remove the toothpicks from the dates, arrange them on a serving platter and drizzle with glaze.

Serve warm.

BACON DEVILED EGGS 3 WAYS

Deviled eggs have come a long way since the cocktail parties and barbecues of the 1950s. They are such a versatile protein powerhouse and a low-carb favorite that you don't need to wait for a party to make these. The salty crispness of bacon is such a perfect complement to the tender eggs that you won't eat deviled eggs by themselves ever again.

Makes 24

For the eggs:
12 large eggs
1   teaspoon baking soda
6   slices cooked bacon

For Classic Filling:
1½ tablespoons mayonnaise or Bacon Mayonnaise (page 84)
1   teaspoon Dijon mustard
1   teaspoon apple cider vinegar
1   teaspoon minced chives
⅛   teaspoon salt
⅛   teaspoon freshly ground black pepper
2   dashes hot sauce

For Curry Filling:
2½ tablespoons mayonnaise or Bacon Mayonnaise (page 84)
1   teaspoon apple cider vinegar
½   teaspoon curry powder
½   teaspoon chopped parsley
⅛   teaspoon salt

For Green Filling:
¼   avocado, mashed
2   tablespoons mayonnaise or Bacon Mayonnaise (page 84)
1   teaspoon apple cider vinegar
½   teaspoon minced shallots
½   teaspoon finely chopped cilantro
⅛   teaspoon salt
⅛   teaspoon freshly ground black pepper

In a large pot, place eggs in a single layer. Fill the pot with water until the eggs are covered by at least 1 inch of water. Add baking soda to the pot. Bring to a full boil, uncovered, and boil eggs for 1 minute. Cover the pot and remove from heat. Allow the eggs to sit, covered, for 10 minutes. Meanwhile prepare an ice bath by filling a large bowl with ice and cold water. After 10 minutes, remove the eggs from the pot and place them in the ice bath. Allow eggs to cool for at least 5 minutes. To remove the shells gently tap and roll the eggs on the counter and peel the shells. Rinse under cold water and keep refrigerated until ready to use. The eggs can be made up to 3 days ahead of time.

Slice eggs lengthwise. Remove egg yolks and divide evenly among three small mixing bowls. Each bowl should have four whole egg yolks.

For the Classic Filling, add mayonnaise, mustard, vinegar, chives, salt, pepper, and hot sauce to cooked egg yolks. Mash and stir with a fork or the back of a spoon until smooth.

For the Curry Filling, add mayonnaise, vinegar, curry powder, chopped parsley, and salt to cooked egg yolks. Mash and stir with a fork or the back of a spoon until smooth.

For the Green Filling, add mashed avocado, mayonnaise, vinegar, shallots, chopped cilantro, salt, and pepper to cooked egg yolks. Mash and stir with a fork or the back of a spoon until smooth.

Fill each cooked egg white with a heaping spoonful of each filling. Each filling will make eight egg white halves. Break bacon slices into 1-inch to 2-inch pieces. Depending on the length of your bacon you will need at least 24 pieces. Top each egg half with cooked bacon pieces and serve.

THE LOVE ME TENDER SANDWICH

Say what you will about Elvis and his famous mega-calorie sandwich creation, but this one is a must try. Fried in Maple Bacon Butter with the addition of chocolate-hazelnut spread, this version is even more of a good thing than the original.

Makes 1 sandwich

For the Maple Bacon Butter
8   tablespoons (1 stick) unsalted butter, softened
2   tablespoons minced cooked bacon
1   tablespoon maple syrup
1/8 teaspoon salt

For the Sandwich:
2   slices brioche bread
2   slices cooked bacon
1/2 large banana, sliced lengthwise
2   tablespoons creamy peanut butter
1   tablespoon chocolate-hazelnut spread

In a food processor, combine butter, maple syrup, and salt until smooth. Add minced bacon and pulse until just combined.

Spread 1 tablespoon of Maple Bacon Butter on one side of each slice of brioche bread. Flip bread slices over. Spread 2 tablespoons peanut butter on one of the bread slices, top with cooked bacon, and the banana slices. Spread 1 tablespoon of chocolate-hazelnut spread on the other slice of bread. Place this bread slice, chocolate side down, on top of banana and bacon slices. Press gently to adhere.

Cook sandwiches in a non-stick skillet over medium heat until golden brown, about 2 minutes per side. Serve warm.

BAKED POTATO SKINS

For best results, bake the potatoes in the oven. If you cheat and use the microwave, the skins don't seem to come out as crisp. Serve these as a side dish to grilled steak or barbecued chicken.

Makes 8

4   Russet potatoes
½   cup bacon, cooked and crumbled (about 6 slices)
2   cups sour cream
1   (1-ounce) package ranch dressing mix
1¼   cups shredded Cheddar, divided
2   tablespoons thinly sliced chives

Preheat oven to 450°F. Wash and dry the potatoes, and pierce the skins all over with a fork. Bake the potatoes directly on the oven rack until they are tender and the skins are crisp, about 1 hour.

In a medium bowl, whisk together the sour cream, ranch dressing mix, crumbled bacon, and 1 cup of the Cheddar.

Remove the cooked potatoes from the oven and reduce the oven temperature to 350°F. While the potatoes are still hot, cut them in half and scoop out the flesh, leaving the skins intact. We like to cut them crosswise so they form nice serving cups. Add the hot potato flesh to the sour cream mixture and blend with a potato masher or electric mixer until evenly combined.

Spoon the sour cream and potato mixture back into the potato skins and arrange the potato halves on a baking sheet. Sprinkle the tops with the remaining cheese.

Bake the potato skins until the cheese is melted and the potatoes are heated through, about 30 minutes.

Garnish with chives and serve hot.

*Over-the-top bacon lover's tip:

Before putting the potatoes in the oven, rub the skins with a little Clarified Bacon Fat (page 22).

BACON
CHEESE PUFFS

These buttery, airy spheres of perfection will go so fast you will have to fight to sample the fruits of your labor. They are super simple to make and many of the ingredients are common staples, so you may find yourself making them quite often. Comté is a rich, nutty cave-aged French cheese. You can also substitute Parmesan or sharp Cheddar.

Makes about 24 cheese puffs

½	cup water
4	tablespoons (½ stick) unsalted butter, cut into cubes
¼	teaspoon salt
½	cup all-purpose flour
2	large eggs
¾	cup shredded Comté, divided (about 3 ounces)
⅓	cup cooked and crumbled peppered bacon (about 4 slices)
2	teaspoons chopped fresh herbs, such as chives, thyme, and/or marjoram

Preheat the oven to 425°F.

Line a baking sheet with parchment paper.

In a medium saucepan, combine the water, butter, and salt. Heat the pan over medium heat until the butter is melted and the water just begins to boil. Add the flour all at once and stir vigorously with a wooden spoon until the dough comes together in a ball that pulls away from the sides of the pan, about 3 minutes. Test the dough by giving the pan a few good shakes. If the ball stays together, it is done.

Transfer the dough to the bowl of an electric mixer. Cool for 5 minutes. Beat the dough at low speed with the paddle attachment, while adding the eggs, one at a time. Make sure the first egg is fully incorporated before adding the second. The finished dough should be smooth and shiny. Stir in ½ cup of the shredded cheese, the bacon, and herbs.

Transfer the dough to a pastrybag fitted with a ½-inch-wide plain tip. Pipe the dough onto the parchment lined baking sheet in 1-inch mounds about 2 inches apart. Use the back of a spoon dipped in water to pat down any pointed tips. Sprinkle with the remaining cheese.

Bake for 10 minutes at 425°F, then reduce oven temperature to 375°F and bake for an additional 20 to 25 minutes, or until the cheese puffs are a deep, golden brown.

Serve warm.

*Over-the-top bacon lover's tip:

Brush mounds of dough with a little melted Clarified Bacon Fat (page 22) before sprinkling with remaining cheese and baking.

Candied Bacon

CANDIED BACON S'MORES

This little gem may have your friends around the campfire gasping with delight. Candied bacon is light and sturdy enough to pack into even remote locations. Bacon-laced bars of dark chocolate are available at many gourmet stores. If camping isn't your thing, these can also be made at home by toasting the marshmallows over a burner and warming the assembled s'mores to drippy perfection in the oven.

Makes 4

4   jumbo marshmallows
4   (2-inch) pieces of Candied Bacon (recipe follows)
4   graham crackers, halved
4   (2-inch) squares dark chocolate, such as Vosges Bacon Chocolate brand

Roast the marshmallows over an open flame until golden brown, puffed, and gooey on the inside. Sandwich the warm marshmallows with the candied bacon and chocolate between layers of graham crackers.

Serve immediately.

CANDIED BACON

Makes 12 slices

½   cup granulated sugar
½   cup light brown sugar
1   tablespoon cinnamon
12 slices thick-cut bacon

Preheat oven to 375°F. Arrange a wire rack over a foil-lined baking sheet.

In a medium bowl, combine the sugar, brown sugar, and cinnamon. Add the bacon slices and toss to coat.

Place the sugar-coated bacon slices on wire rack and bake, flipping once, until the bacon is crisp and the sugar is caramelized, 25 to 30 minutes. Cool slightly on rack before removing.

Serve immediately or store in an airtight container in the refrigerator for up to 1 week.

CARDAMOM CUPCAKES WITH MAPLE, BACON, AND CREAM CHEESE FROSTING

These cupcakes have a lovely balance of spice and sweetness. But let's face it, it's the frosting that really counts when it comes to cupcakes. Our Maple, Bacon, and Cream Cheese version is a showstopper on virtually any cupcake flavor, including classic vanilla, carrot cake, or chocolate.

Makes 12 cupcakes

- 1⅓ cups all-purpose flour
- 1¼ teaspoons baking powder
- 1 teaspoon ground cardamom
- ½ teaspoon ground ginger
- ¼ teaspoon grated nutmeg
- ¼ teaspoon salt
- ⅛ teaspoon ground cloves
- ½ cup (1 stick) unsalted butter, softened
- ⅓ cup granulated sugar
- ⅓ cup lightly packed, dark brown sugar
- 2 large eggs
- ½ teaspoon vanilla extract
- ½ cup buttermilk
- Maple, Bacon, and Cream Cheese Frosting (page 175)

Preheat oven to 350°F. Fill a 12-cup cupcake pan with paper liners.

Sift together the flour, baking powder, cardamom, ginger, nutmeg, and salt. Sift onto a large sheet of wax or parchment paper to make pouring it into the mixing bowl more convenient.

In the bowl of an electric mixer, whip the butter and sugars together until light and fluffy, about 3 minutes on medium-high speed. Add the eggs one at a time, waiting until each egg is fully incorporated before adding the next and scraping down the sides of the bowl after each addition. Add the vanilla. Reduce the mixer speed slightly and alternate adding the dry ingredients and the buttermilk, beginning and ending with the dry ingredients.

Divide the batter evenly among the cupcake pan, filling each cup with about ⅓ cup of the batter. Bake the cupcakes until a cake-tester comes out clean when inserted near the center, 18 to 22 minutes. For even cooking, rotate the cupcake pan halfway through the baking time. Cool the cupcakes for 5 minutes in the pan, then transfer them to a rack and cool completely.

Frost with Maple, Bacon, and Cream Cheese Frosting.

MAPLE, BACON, AND CREAM CHEESE FROSTING

Makes 3 cups, to frost 12 cupcakes

1	(8-ounce) package cream cheese, softened
½	cup (1 stick) unsalted butter, softened
2	tablespoons pure maple syrup
2	cups powdered sugar, sifted
¼	cup chopped, toasted pecans
¼	cup cooked and crumbled bacon (about 3 slices)

In an electric mixer beat the cream cheese and butter on medium speed until smooth and evenly combined. Add the maple syrup. With mixer on low, gradually add the powdered sugar until the frosting is thick and spreadable. Fold in the toasted pecans and bacon bits.

BACON CASHEW CARAMEL CORN

This is a very special caramel corn, so save it for very special movie nights or events. Or, put it in a decorative container or gift bag and give it away for the holidays. Substitute brandy or Cognac for the apple brandy if it is unavailable. We suggest that you pop the corn in a hot-air style popper, or microwave the kernels in plain brown lunch bags for about 3 minutes on high. Work in batches, using only 2 tablespoons of popcorn kernels per bag.

Makes about 14 cups

12 cups of popped corn (made from about ½ cup popcorn kernels)
1 cup cooked and crumbled bacon (about 12 slices)
1 cup roasted, salted cashews
1 cup granulated sugar
4 tablespoons (½ stick) unsalted butter
¼ cup water
2 tablespoons light corn syrup
¼ cup heavy cream
1 ounce (2 tablespoons) Calvados or other apple brandy
1 teaspoon fleur de sel

Preheat oven to 300°F.

In a very large bowl, toss together the popped corn, bacon bits, and cashews.

Line a sheet pan with foil and brush evenly with oil.

Stir the sugar, butter, water, and corn syrup together in a saucepan. Continue stirring over medium heat until the sugar dissolves and butter is melted. Increase the temperature to medium-high and boil, without stirring, until the syrup turns a deep amber color, about 13 minutes. While the syrup cooks, you may want to carefully swirl the pan and brush down the sides carefully with a wet pastry brush to prevent any sugar crystals from forming, but do not stir.

Remove the syrup from the heat and immediately pour in the cream. Protect your face and hands, as there will be a lot of steam and the syrup will bubble violently. Add the Calvados and stir until well blended. Immediately pour the hot caramel mixture over the popcorn mixture and toss with a large spoon or spatula coated with oil until evenly mixed. Transfer the mixture to the oiled sheet pan.

Bake the caramel corn for 20 minutes, tossing every few minutes for even crispness. Sprinkle with fleur de sel. Cool completely and transfer to an airtight container until ready to serve.

*Over-the-top bacon lover's tip:

Pop popcorn in Clarified Bacon Fat (page 22) on the stovetop.

BACON BAKLAVA

How can those delicate layers of pastry and nuts possibly be improved upon, except with bacon? Phyllo dough can seem scary at first, but once you understand that the sheer quantity of layers will mask the flaws of any individual sheet, you will gain confidence. Orange flower water and rose water are available at gourmet shops and Mediterranean markets.

Makes about 24 servings

½   pound raw walnut pieces
½   pound raw pistachio meats
1   cup cooked and crumbled bacon (about 12 slices)
⅓   cup granulated sugar
1   teaspoon ground cardamom
1¼   cup (2½ sticks) unsalted butter, melted
1   (16-ounce) package phyllo dough, thawed
1   cup water
1   cup granulated sugar
1   cup honey
1   cinnamon stick
¼   cup orange flower water or rose water

Preheat oven to 350°F

In a food processor, pulse the nuts until they are ground, but not turned into meal. Add the bacon, sugar, and cardamom and pulse a few more times until the nut mixture is finely chopped and evenly blended.

Begin layering the baklava. Brush a jellyroll pan, or sheet pan with sides, generously with the melted butter. Unroll the phyllo dough and cover the sheets with a piece of plastic wrap and a damp towel. This keeps the sheets from drying out while you are layering the baklava. Read the package for detailed handling instructions.

Place a sheet of phyllo on the sheet pan and brush it with melted butter. Repeat with six more sheets of phyllo dough and butter for a total of seven sheets. You do not have to cover every last inch of the phyllo with butter, but try and have it evenly dispersed between all of the layers. Spread ⅓ cup of the nut mixture evenly over the phyllo. Top the nuts with two more buttered sheets of phyllo. Continue sprinkling with ⅓ cup of the nut mixture adding two sheets of buttered phyllo until all of the nut mixture is used. Top with a final layer of seven buttered phyllo sheets.

Use a sharp knife to cut the uncooked baklava into 24 diamond shapes. Bake the baklava until it is brown and crisp, 30 to 35 minutes.

While the baklava is baking, combine the water, sugar, and honey in a saucepan. Gradually heat the mixture until the sugar dissolves. Add the cinnamon stick and bring the mixture to a boil. Reduce the heat slightly and simmer for 25 to 30 minutes. Remove the pan from heat, add the orange flower water and cool slightly. Pour the syrup evenly over the baklava as soon as it comes out of the oven. Make sure you get the syrup in every crack and crevice. Leave to soak for several hours. Serve at room temperature and store leftovers in the refrigerator.

BACON, PEANUT BUTTER, AND CHOCOLATE CHUNK COOKIES

Bacon, peanut butter, and chocolate, it's like a trifecta of bliss. This dough freezes well, so there is no reason why you can't have a batch ready to bake off at any time.

Makes about 24 (3½-inch) cookies

1¼	cups all-purpose flour
¾	teaspoon baking soda
½	teaspoon baking powder
¼	teaspoon salt
½	cup (1 stick) unsalted butter, softened
½	cup granulated sugar
½	cup lightly packed, light brown sugar
½	cup peanut butter
1	large egg
1	teaspoon vanilla extract
½	cup finely chopped roasted, salted peanuts
½	cup semisweet chocolate chunks
¼	cup cooked and crumbled bacon (about 3 slices)

Additional granulated sugar for rolling the cookies

Preheat the oven to 350°F. Line two baking sheets with parchment paper.

Sift together the flour, baking soda, baking powder, and salt. Sift it onto a large sheet of wax or parchment paper to make pouring it into the mixing bowl more convenient.

Beat the butter with an electric mixer on medium-high speed until smooth. Add the sugar and brown sugar, and continue to beat until light and fluffy, 3 to 4 minutes. Beat in the peanut butter until fully incorporated. Beat in the egg and vanilla until thoroughly combined.

Reduce the mixer speed to low and mix in the flour mixture in two additions, scraping down the sides of the bowl as needed. Stir in the peanuts, chocolate chunks, and bacon.

Pour some granulated sugar in a small bowl. Shape the cookie dough into 1½-inch balls. Roll the balls in sugar and place 2 inches apart on the prepared baking sheets. Flatten the cookies with the tines of a fork dipped in cold water to form a crisscross pattern.

Bake the cookies until they are golden brown, 12 to 14 minutes. For best results, rotate the pans front to back and top to bottom halfway through cooking.

Cool the cookies for 2 minutes on the baking sheets before transferring them to a rack to cool completely.

BACON BUTTERMILK CARAMELS

Another great gift idea or a special holiday treat, these caramels have a hint of saltiness and a sophisticated flavor that will please young and old alike.

Makes 48 pieces

⅔   cup hazelnuts
½   cup cooked and crumbled bacon (about 6 slices)
¾   cup buttermilk
¾   cup heavy cream
1½ cups granulated sugar
½   cup lightly packed, light brown sugar
⅓   cup light corn syrup
4   tablespoons (½ stick) unsalted butter
¼   teaspoon salt
1   teaspoon vanilla extract

Preheat oven to 400°F.

Toast the hazelnuts in the oven until the skins are dark and the interiors are lightly browned and fragrant, about 8 minutes. Transfer the nuts to a clean kitchen towel and rub briskly to remove the skins. Chop coarsely.

Spray an 8-by-8-inch square baking pan with cooking spray. Cut two (8-by-15-inch) pieces of parchment paper and lay one vertically and one horizontally in the pan so the pan is fully lined with extra paper coming up over the sides. This will help you remove the caramels from the pan once they are cool. Spray the parchment pieces with cooking spray. Sprinkle the chopped hazelnuts and bacon evenly on the bottom of baking pan. Set aside.

Combine the buttermilk and heavy cream in a large measuring cup. Pour half of the mixed buttermilk and cream into a medium saucepan with the sugar, brown sugar, corn syrup, butter, and salt. Cook over medium heat, stirring constantly, until the sugar is dissolved. Continue to cook without stirring for about 10 minutes.

Stir in the remaining cream mixture and continue to cook until the temperature reaches 250°F on a candy thermometer. Remove the pan from heat and stir in the vanilla, being careful to protect your hands and face from any steam or bubbles. Immediately pour the hot caramel into the prepared pan. Leave to cool completely, at least 1 hour or overnight.

When the caramel is completely cold, lift it out of the pan with the parchment paper. Cut the caramel into 48 equal pieces using a large, lightly oiled knife. Wrap each caramel decoratively with wax paper and string. Store at room temperature for up to 2 weeks.

BACON CRUMB
APPLE PIE

It's almost an American obligation to love apple pie. But we expect apple pie with bacon may become more of a worldwide phenomenon. The apple mixture is boldly spiced to stand up to a streusel topping laced with bacon bits and crystallized ginger. The pastry shell is double baked for crispness. Cover the edges with foil if it is getting too dark while baking.

Makes 1 (9-inch) pie

1   prebaked 9-inch Tender and Flaky Pie Crust (page 29)
2   medium Granny Smith apples, peeled, halved, cored, and thinly sliced
2   medium Braeburn apples, peeled, halved, cored, and thinly sliced
¼   cup lemon juice
1   teaspoon apple cider vinegar
½   teaspoon ground cinnamon
½   teaspoon ground allspice
¼   teaspoon grated nutmeg
½   cup granulated sugar
½   cup lightly packed, light brown sugar
½   cup all-purpose flour
Bacon Streusel (recipe follows)

Preheat oven to 375°F.

Toss together the apple slices, lemon juice, and vinegar in a large bowl. In a small bowl, combine the cinnamon, allspice, nutmeg, sugars, and flour. Toss the apples and spice mixture together to coat.

Fill the prebaked pie crust with the apple mixture and top with Bacon Streusel. Bake until the top is browned and the apples are tender, 50 to 60 minutes. Serve warm or at room temperature

BACON STREUSEL

½   cup all-purpose flour
½   cup light brown sugar
½   cup (1 stick) unsalted butter, very cold
½   cup cooked and crumbled bacon (about 6 slices)
2   tablespoons chopped crystallized ginger

In a medium bowl, combine the flour and brown sugar. Shred the cold butter with a cheese grater into the flour mixture and mix until pea-size clumps form. Add the crumbled bacon and ginger and stir to mix.

If you are not using immediately, store in the refrigerator until ready to use.

INDEX

ACKNOWLEDGMENTS

The creation of this little volume came together because of a team made up of people both inside the Armstrong-Pitts Studios and out.

To start, Theresa Gilliam did an amazing job creating the recipes, and, along with Jean Galton, who edited her recipes, came up with wonderful tasty ways to eat bacon I'd never thought of. Theresa's food styling made every one of her recipes come to life, looking as good as they tasted.

Thanks to Susan Volland for helping us add a bit of wit to copy. We're grateful to Christophe Servieres for his diligent assistance in tracking all things technical, and once again being the "go-to guy" keeping the studio on track and presentable even after several days of bacon grease. The graphic design of this book is the vision of Xiaonan Wang. And we don't know what we'd do without our design mentor Alicia Nammacher, who was there in the trenches with us every step of the way in production and designed the wonderful cover.

A special thanks goes to our ardent supporter and bacon donor, Wilson Winn, who gave us endless supplies of wonderful bacon.

The end thanks goes to the agent for Our Little Book Company— Alison Fargis of Stonesong who kept believing that if she knocked on enough doors to get this published, one would open and eventually it did with the editor of this tome, Ann Treistman from The Countryman Press.

EJ Armstrong

Our Little Book Company
A Black Building Production